Bologna ~ PG Swear Word Coloring Book

Find more amazing coloring books and journals to spark your creativity and get you writing at www.DiaryJournalBook.com.
We'd love to hear from you! Have an idea or something you'd like us to create?
Email us at info@diaryjournalbook.com.
Follow us on Facebook

Everybody gets angry, but not everybody wants to use the crudest of swear words to get their point across. For those of us who can't bring ourselves to cross the line, we opt for the PG version of swearing.

Enjoy blowing off steam by coloring 30 words that won't offend the eyes or other people should they get a hold of your book!

Have fun!

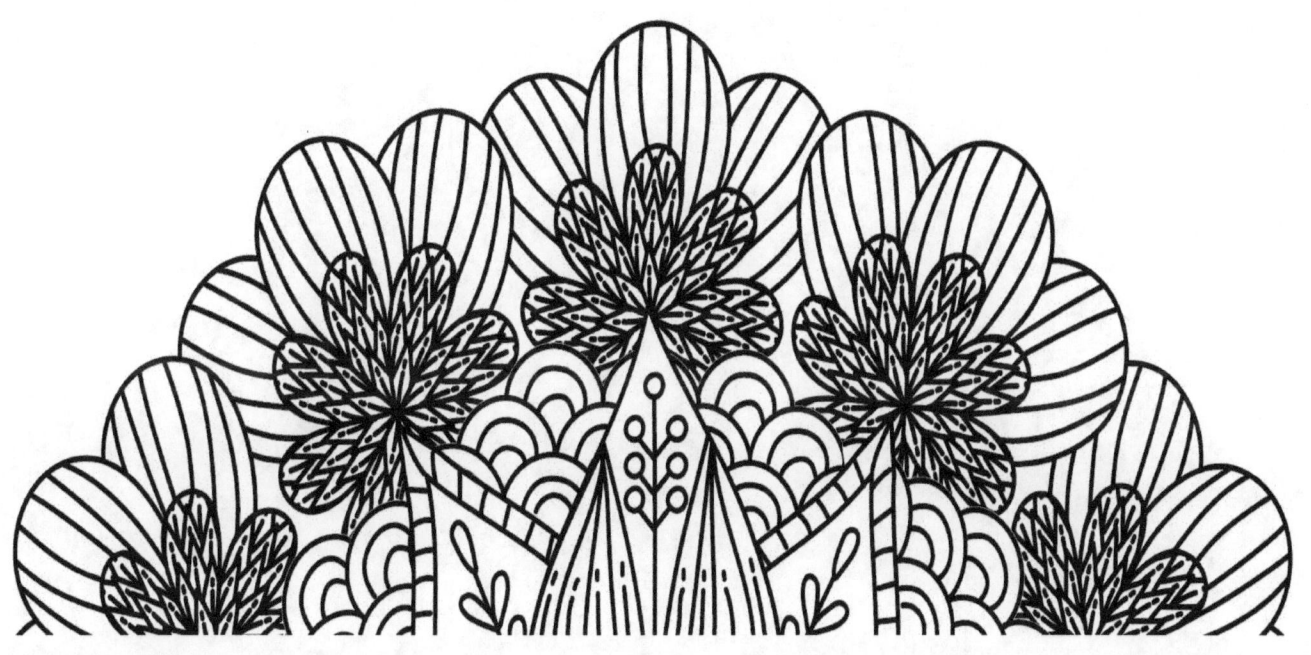

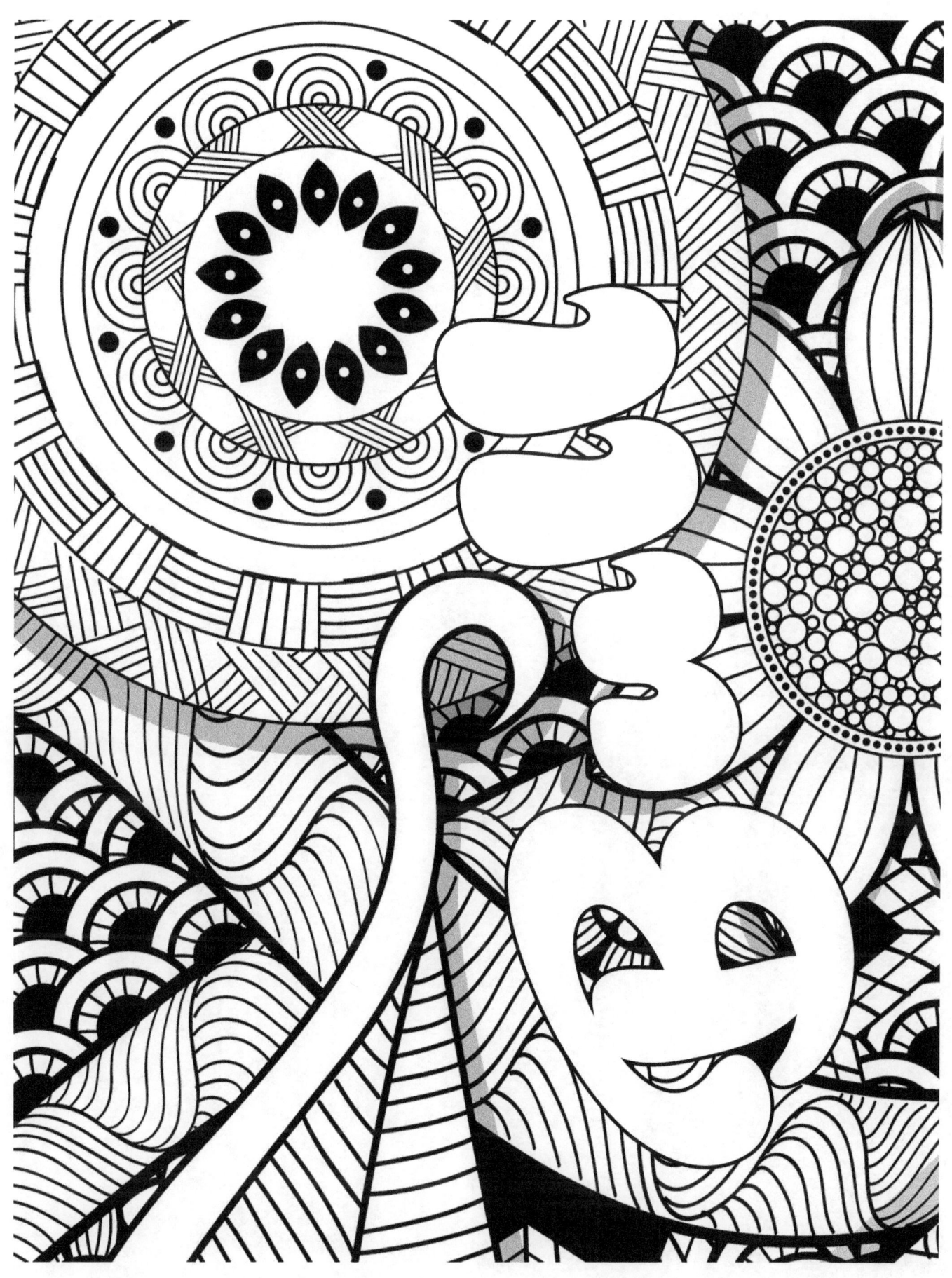

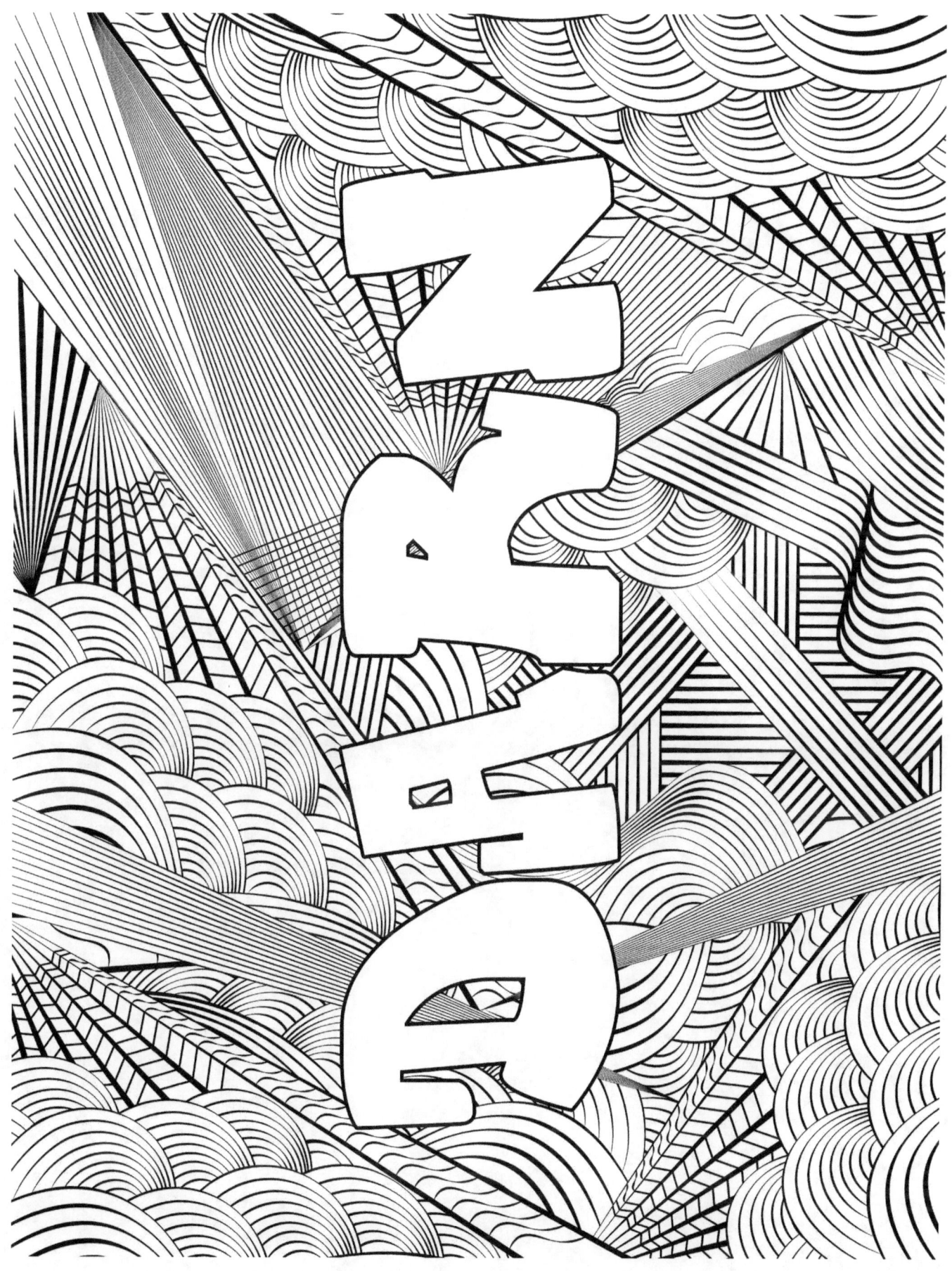

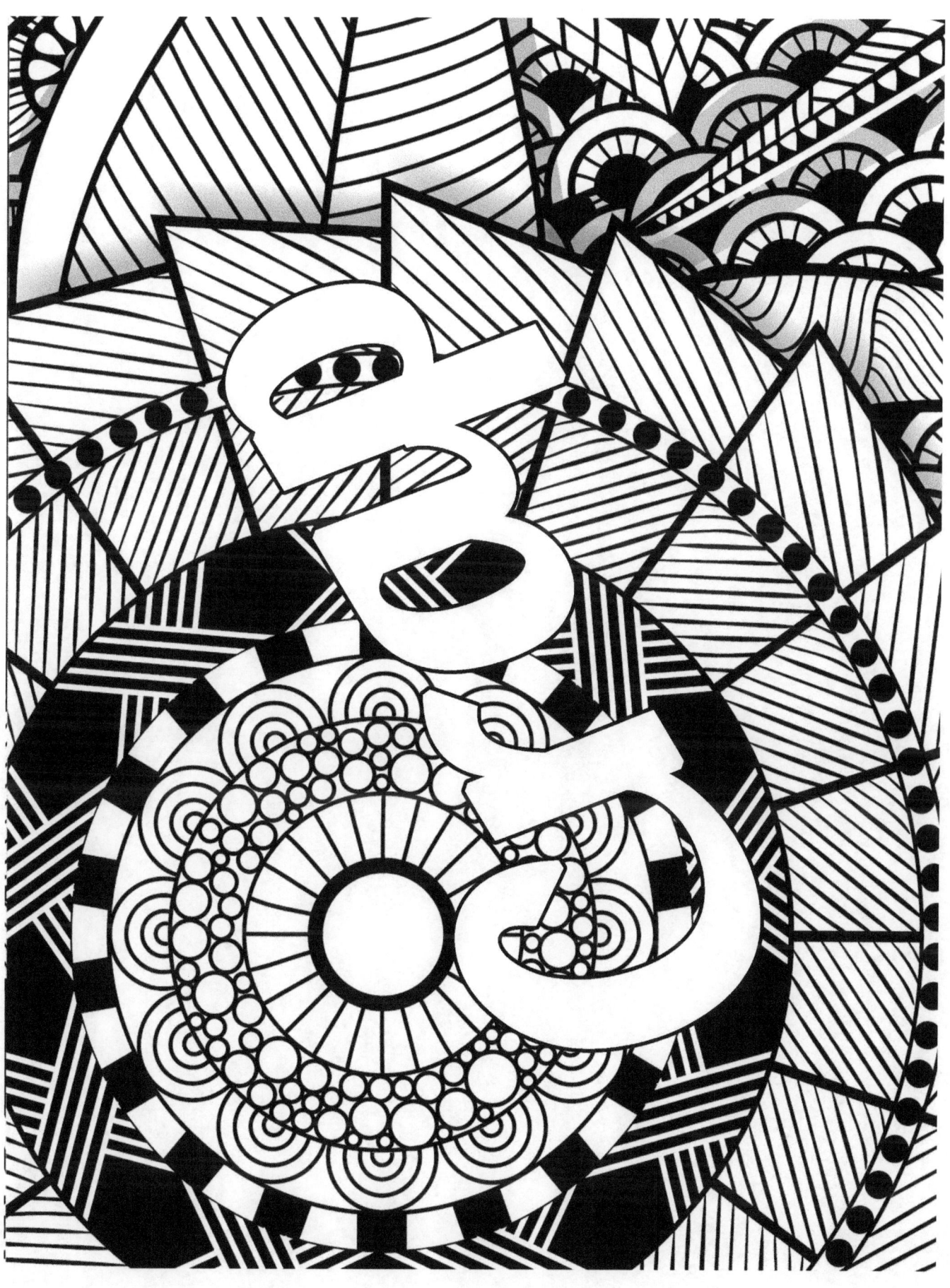

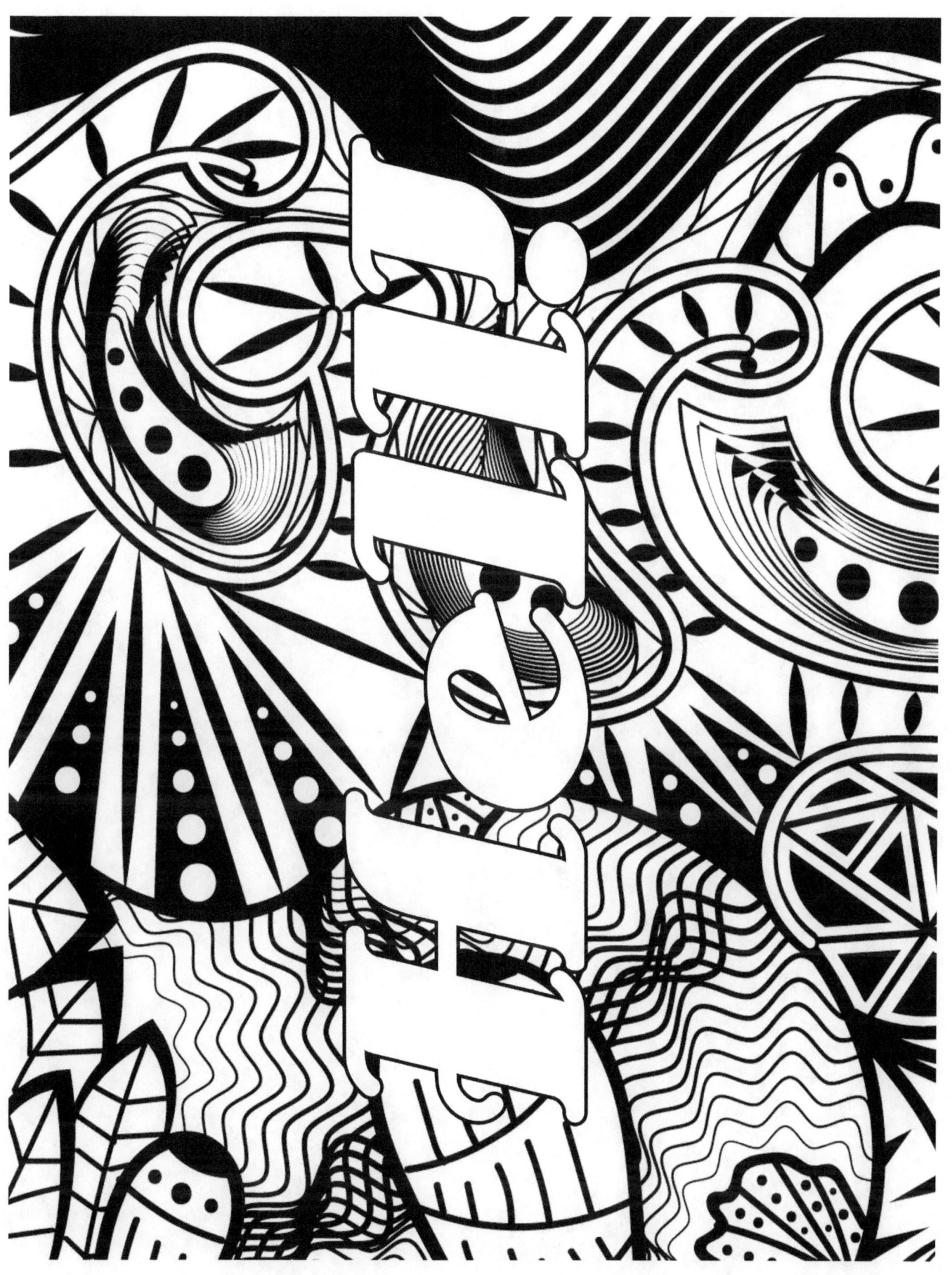

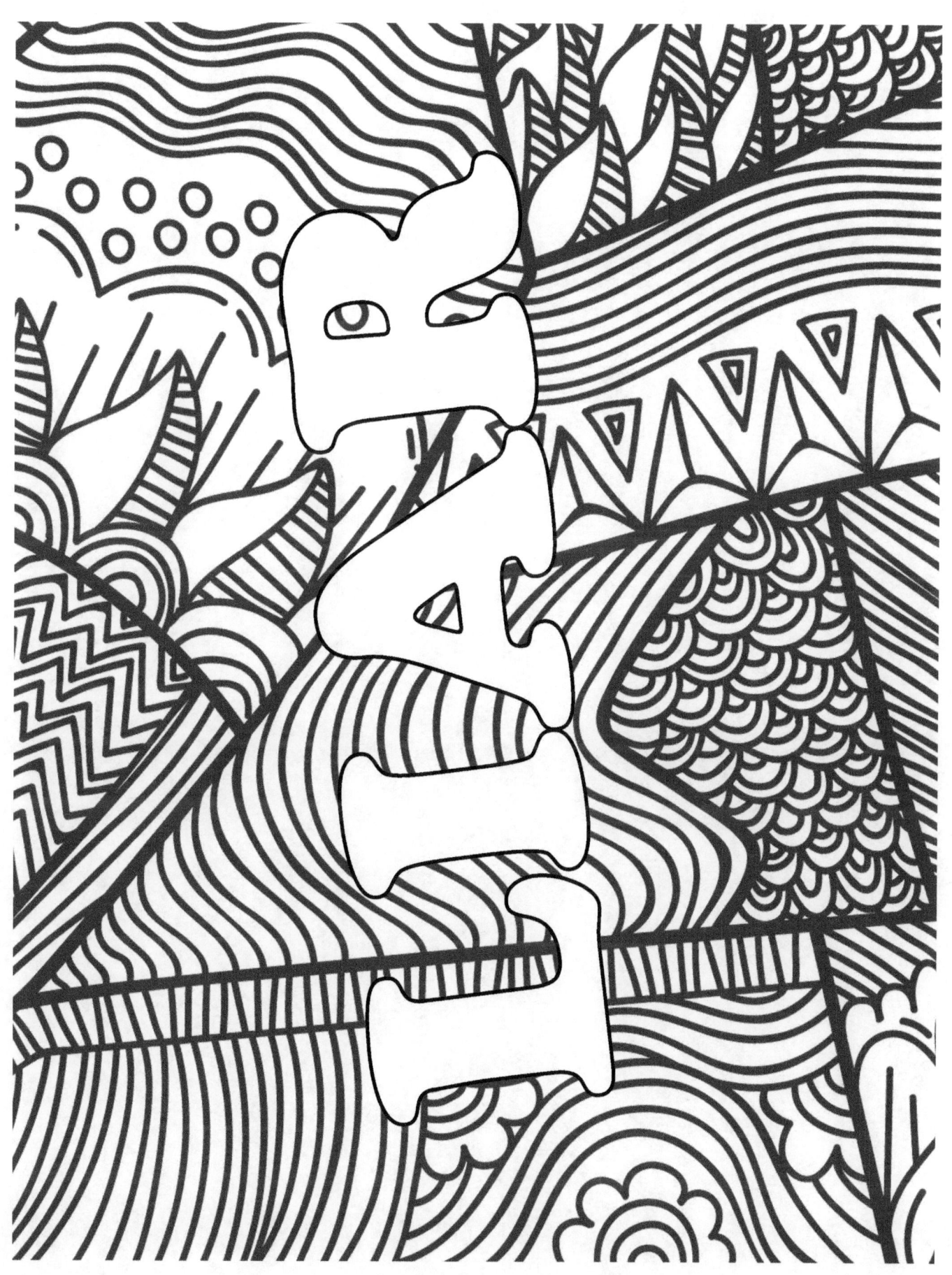

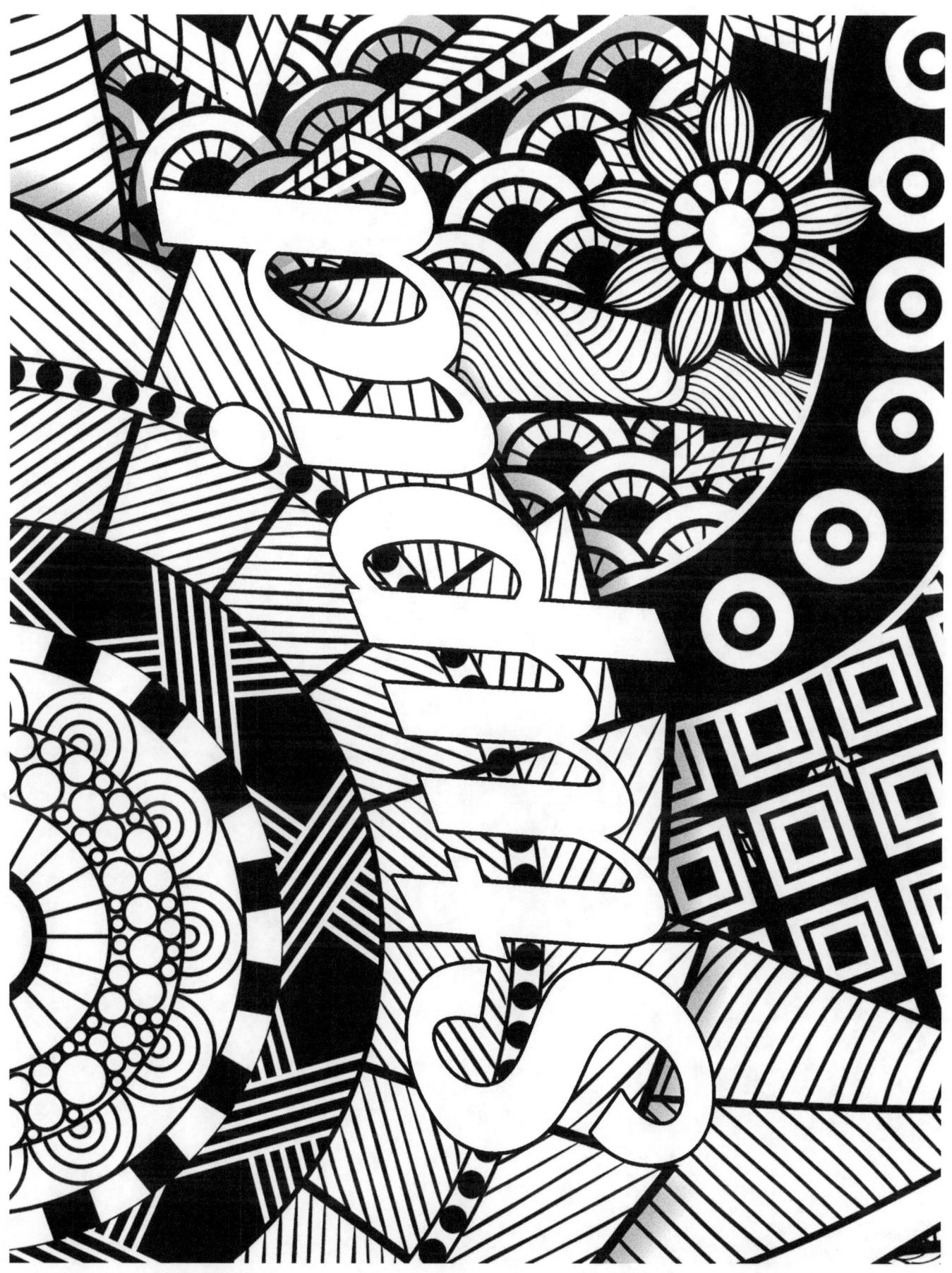

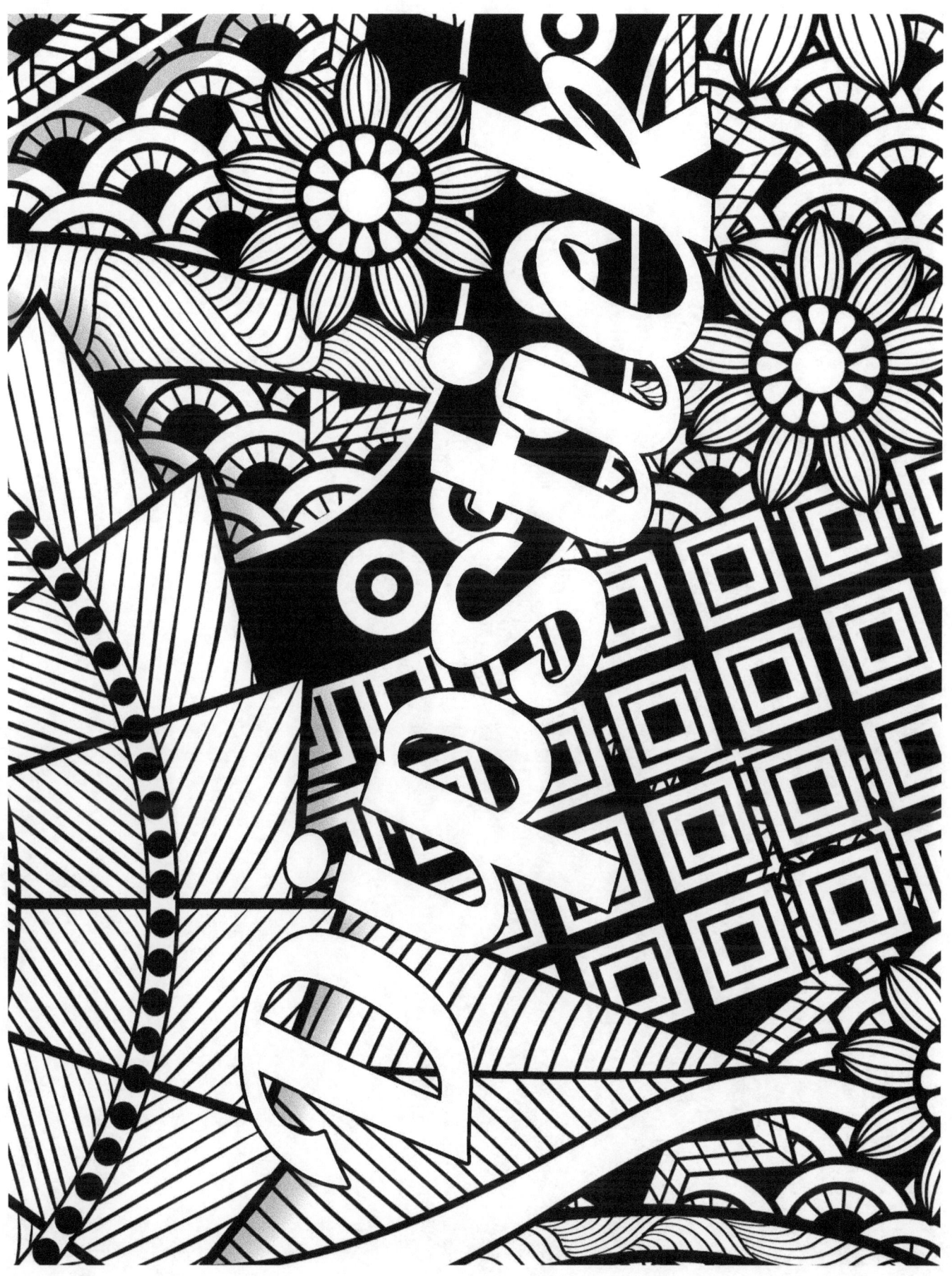

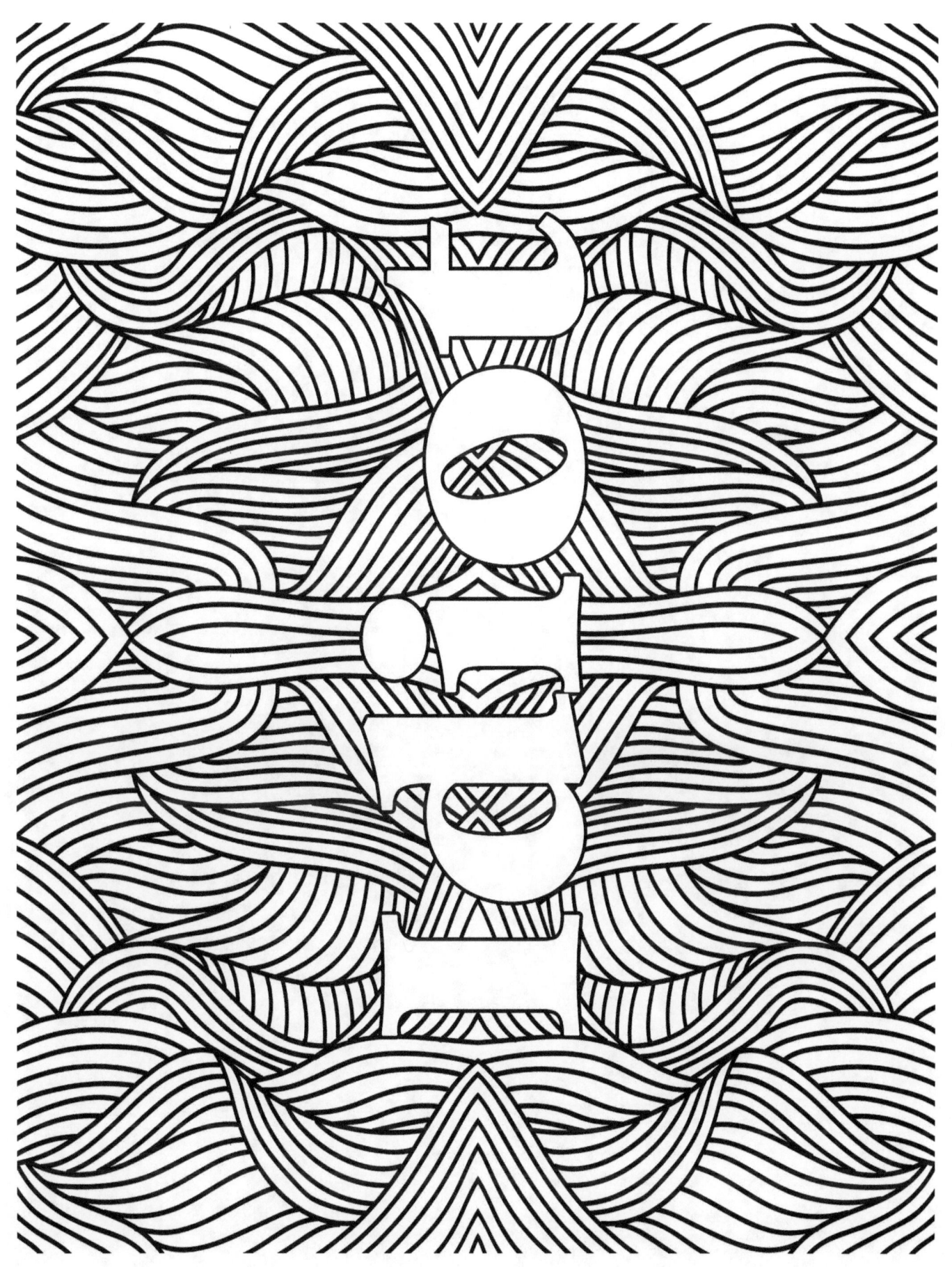

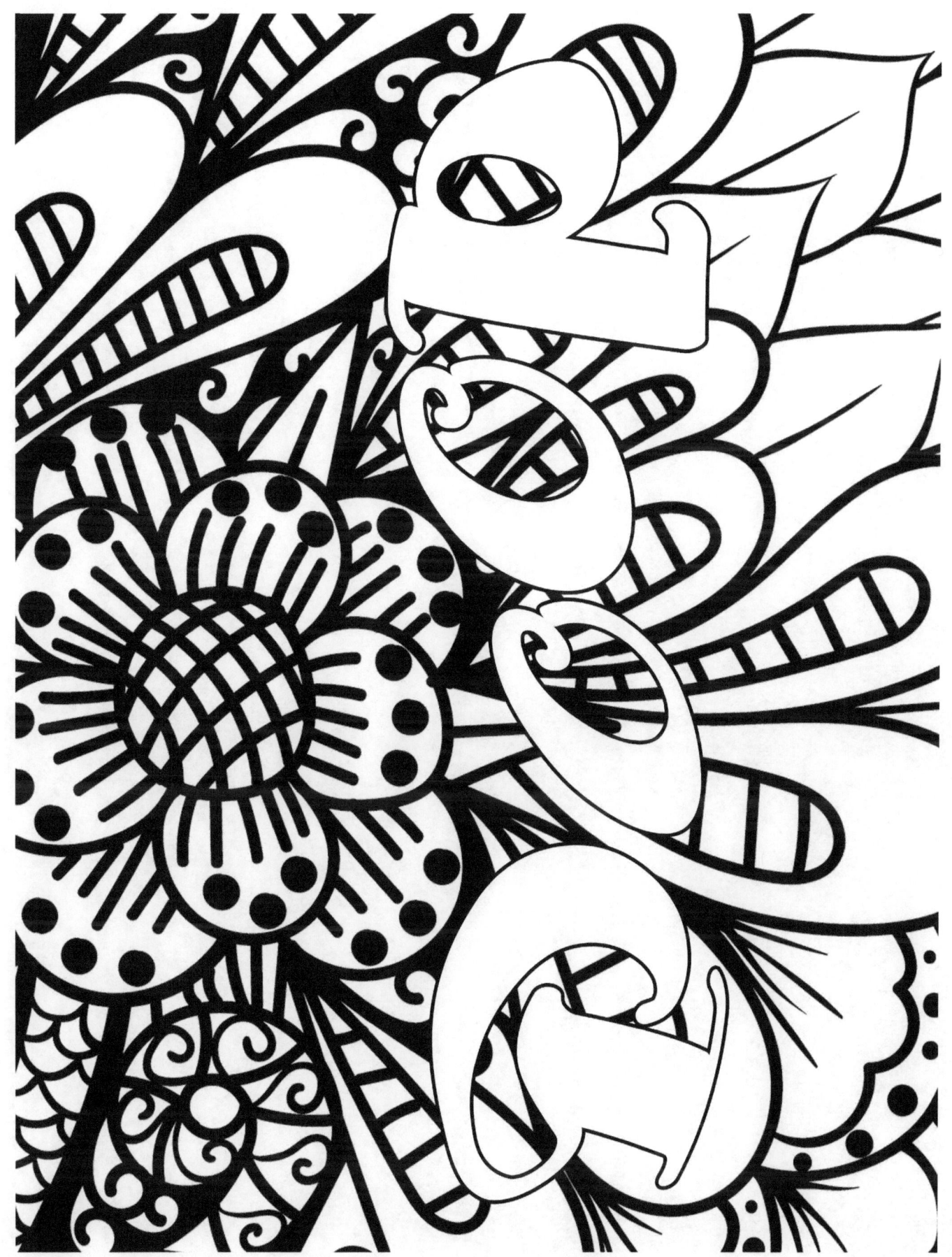

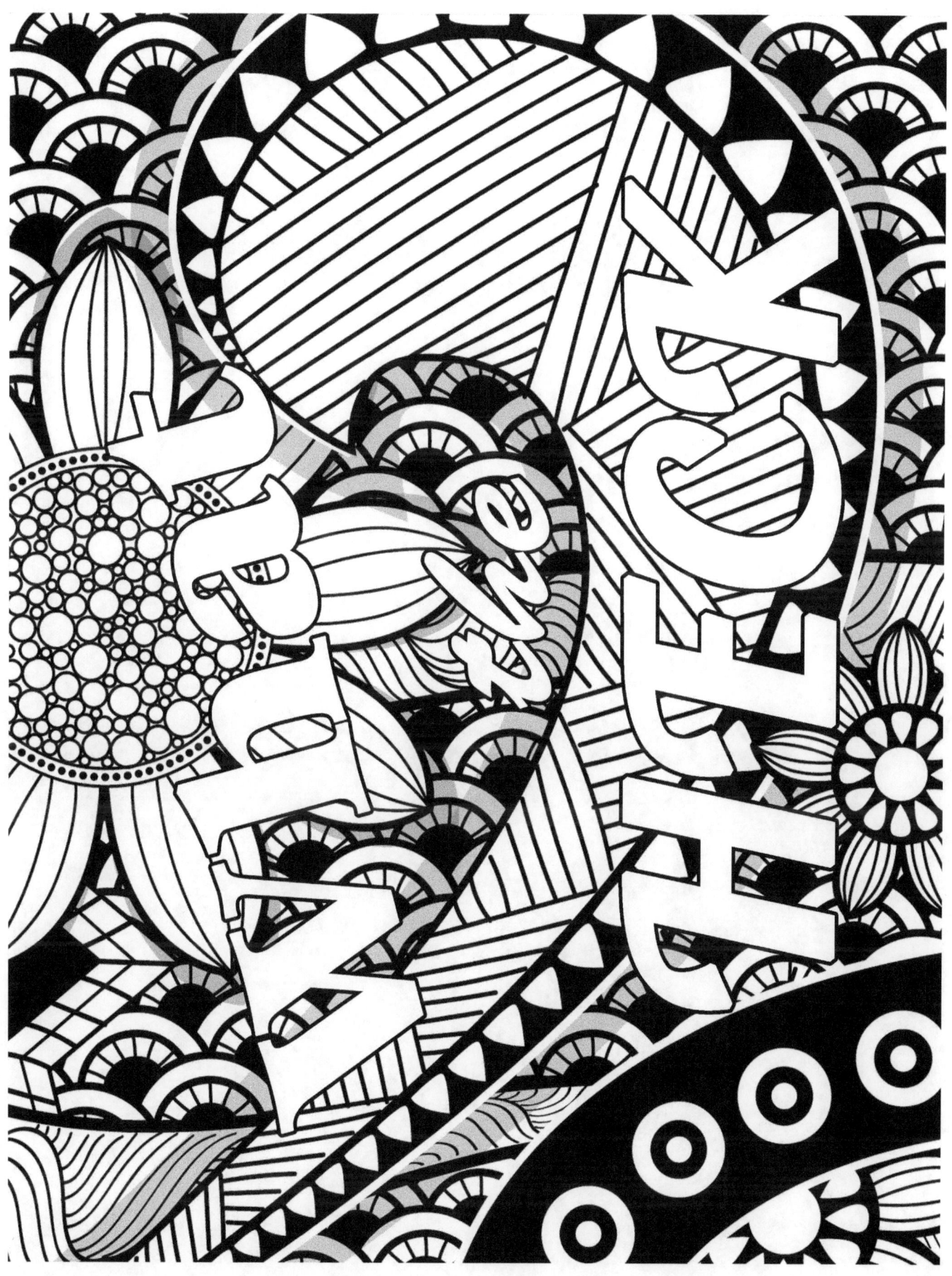

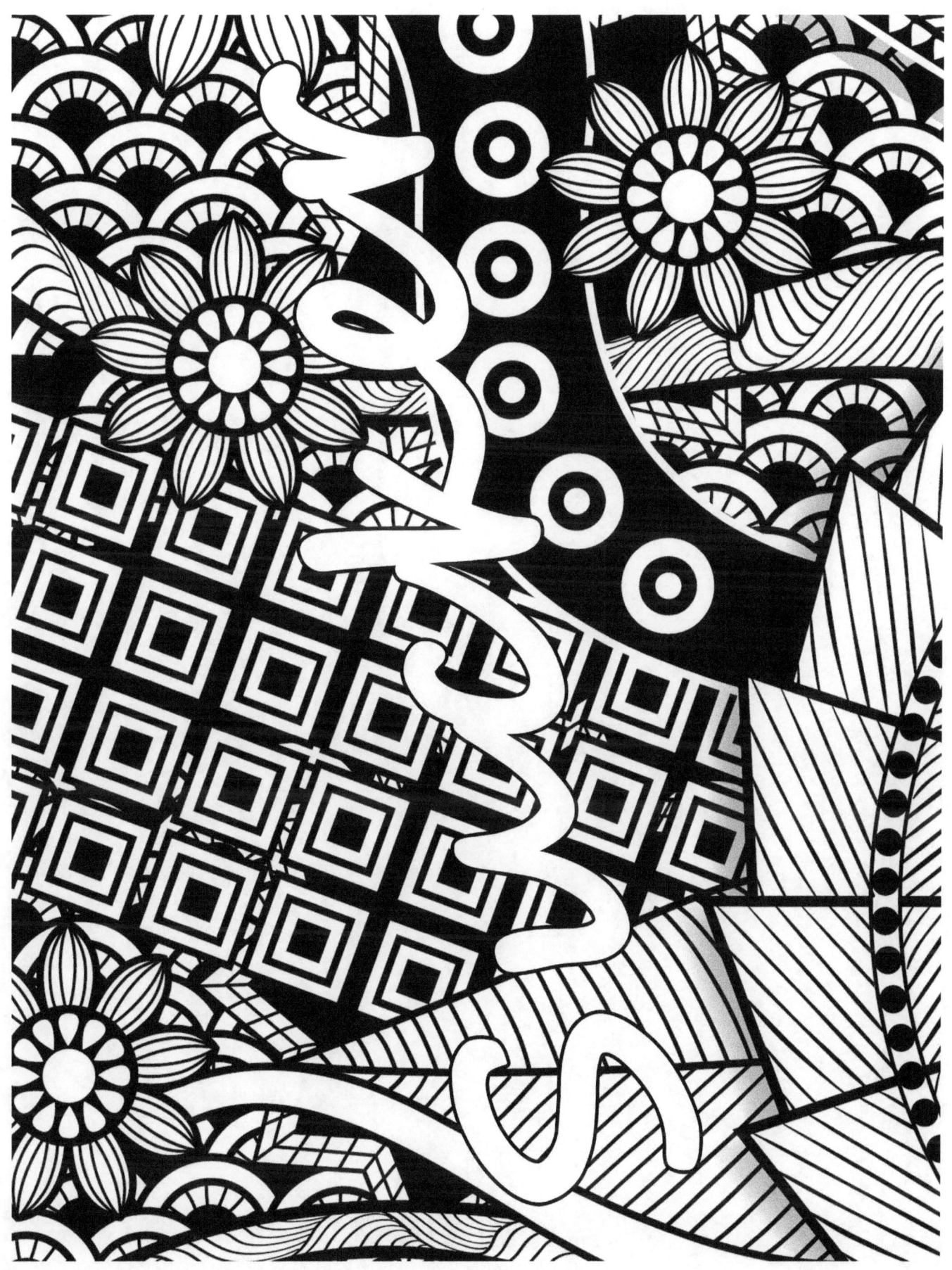

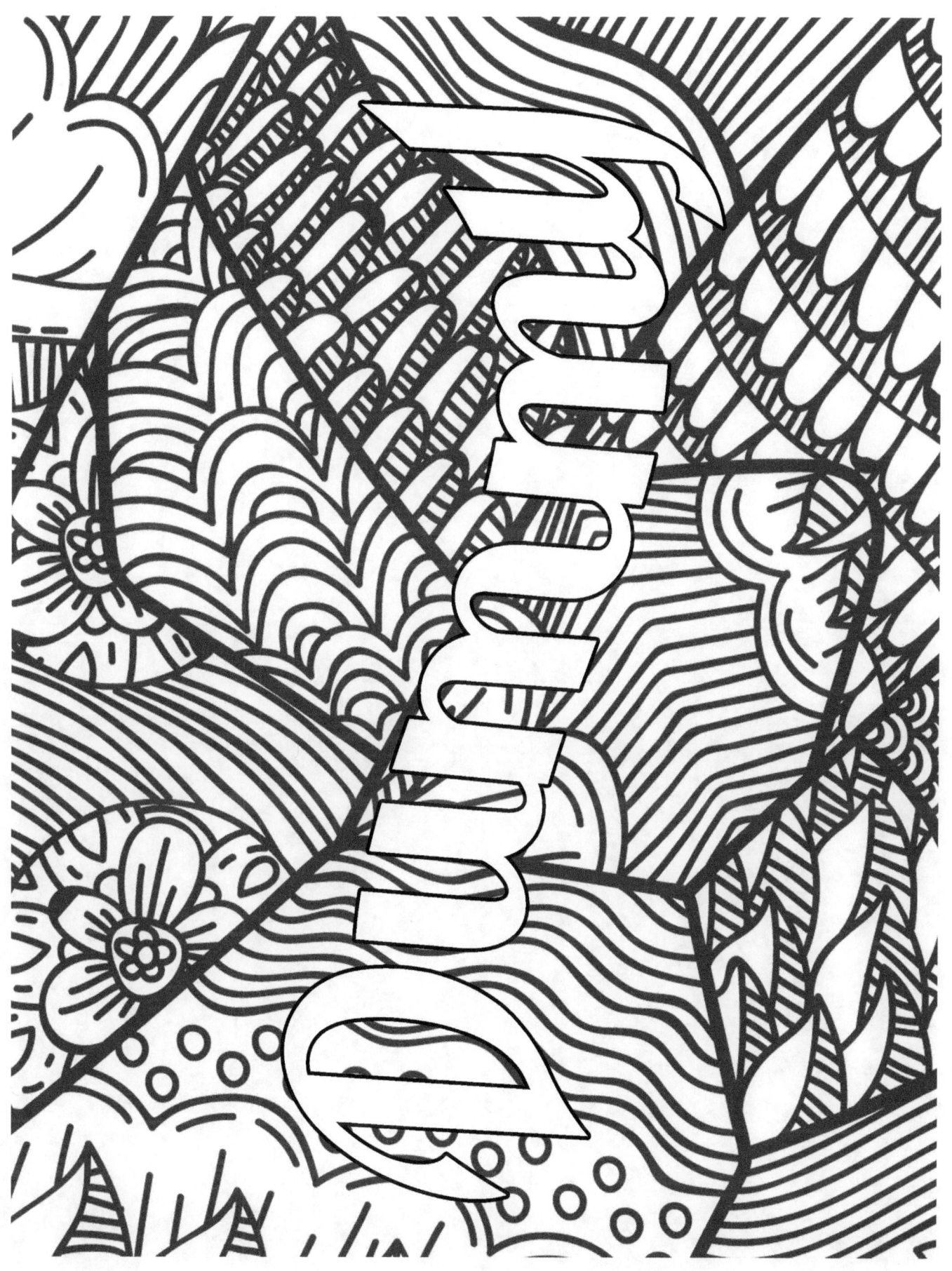

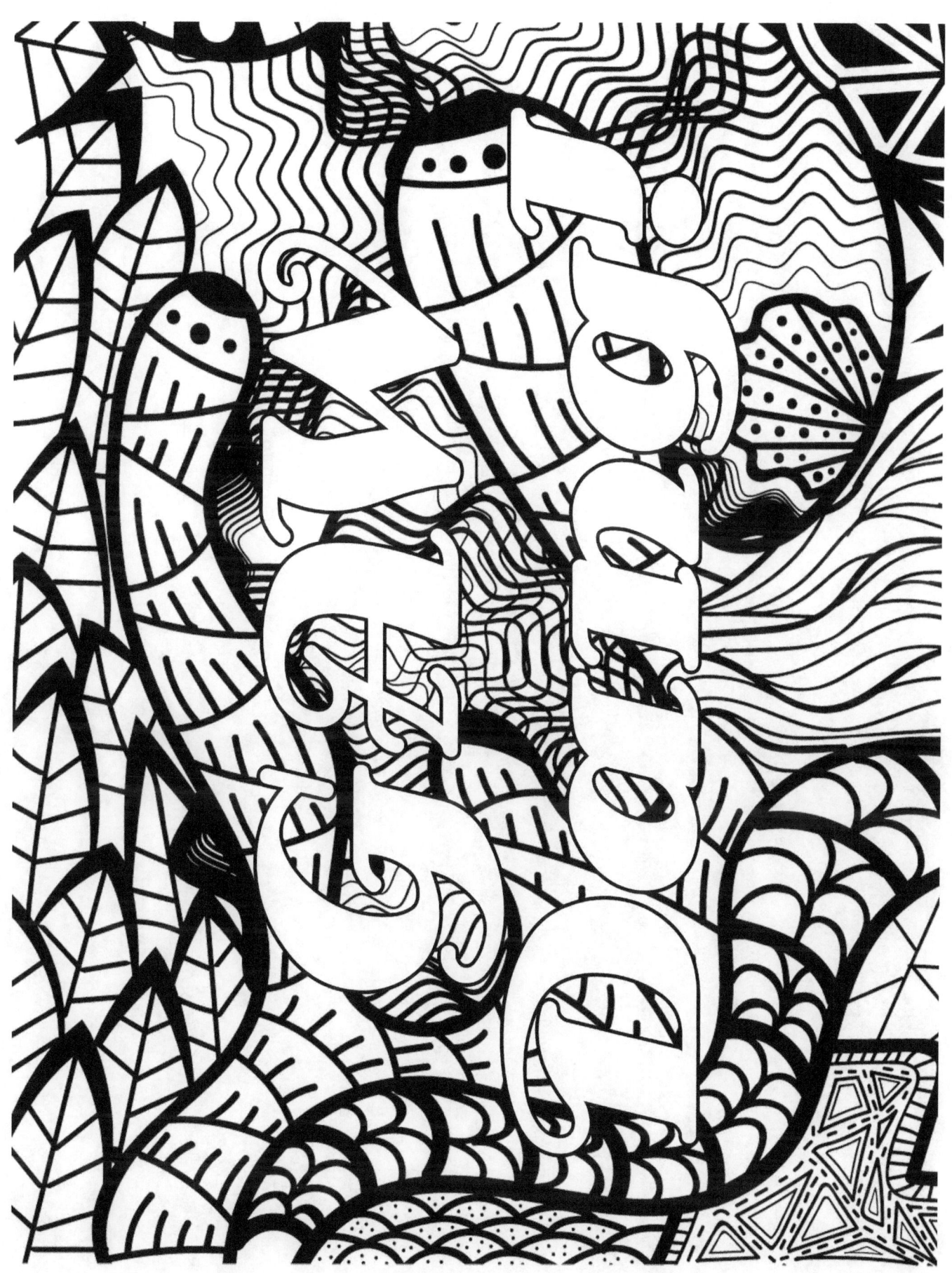

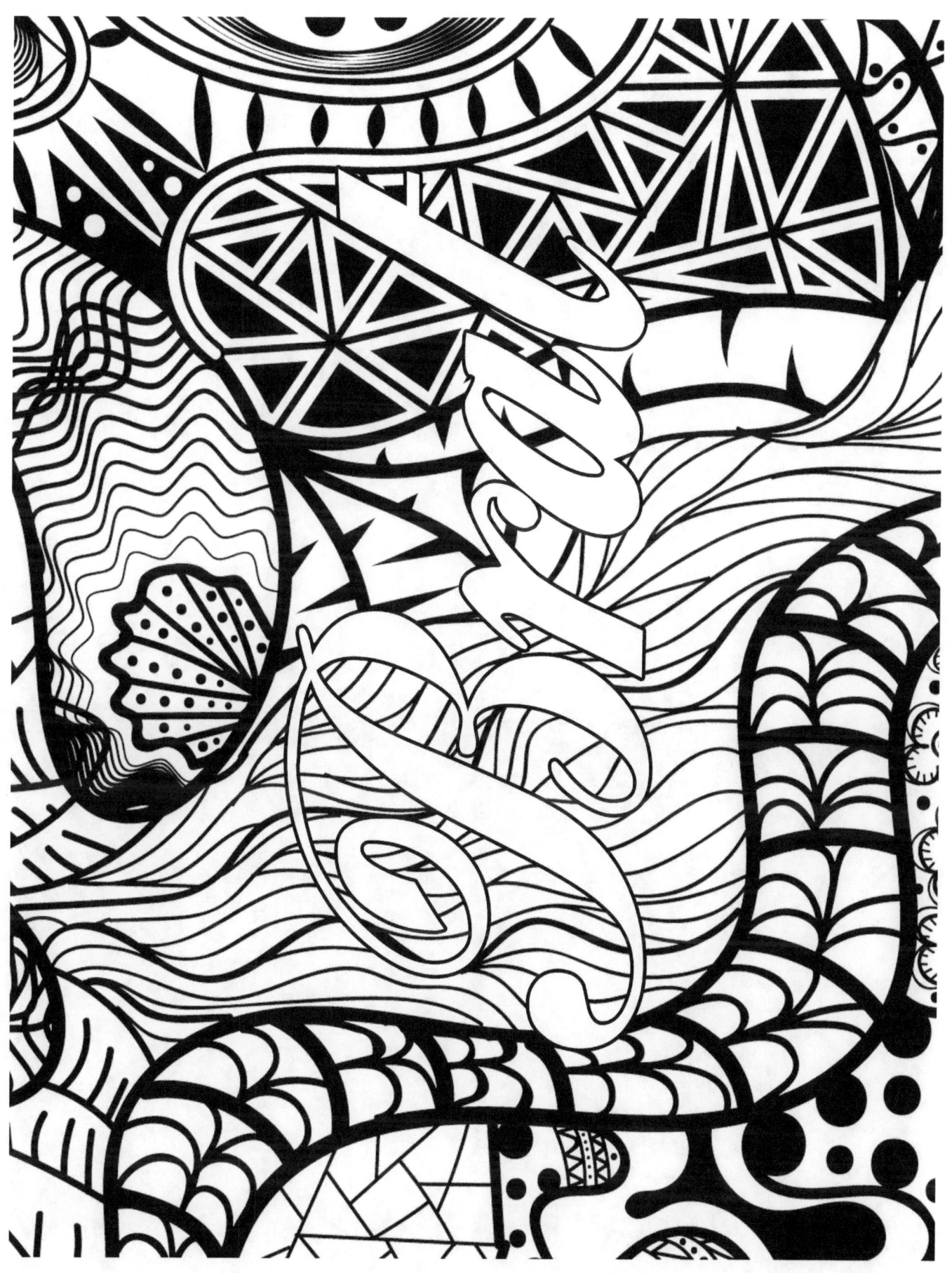

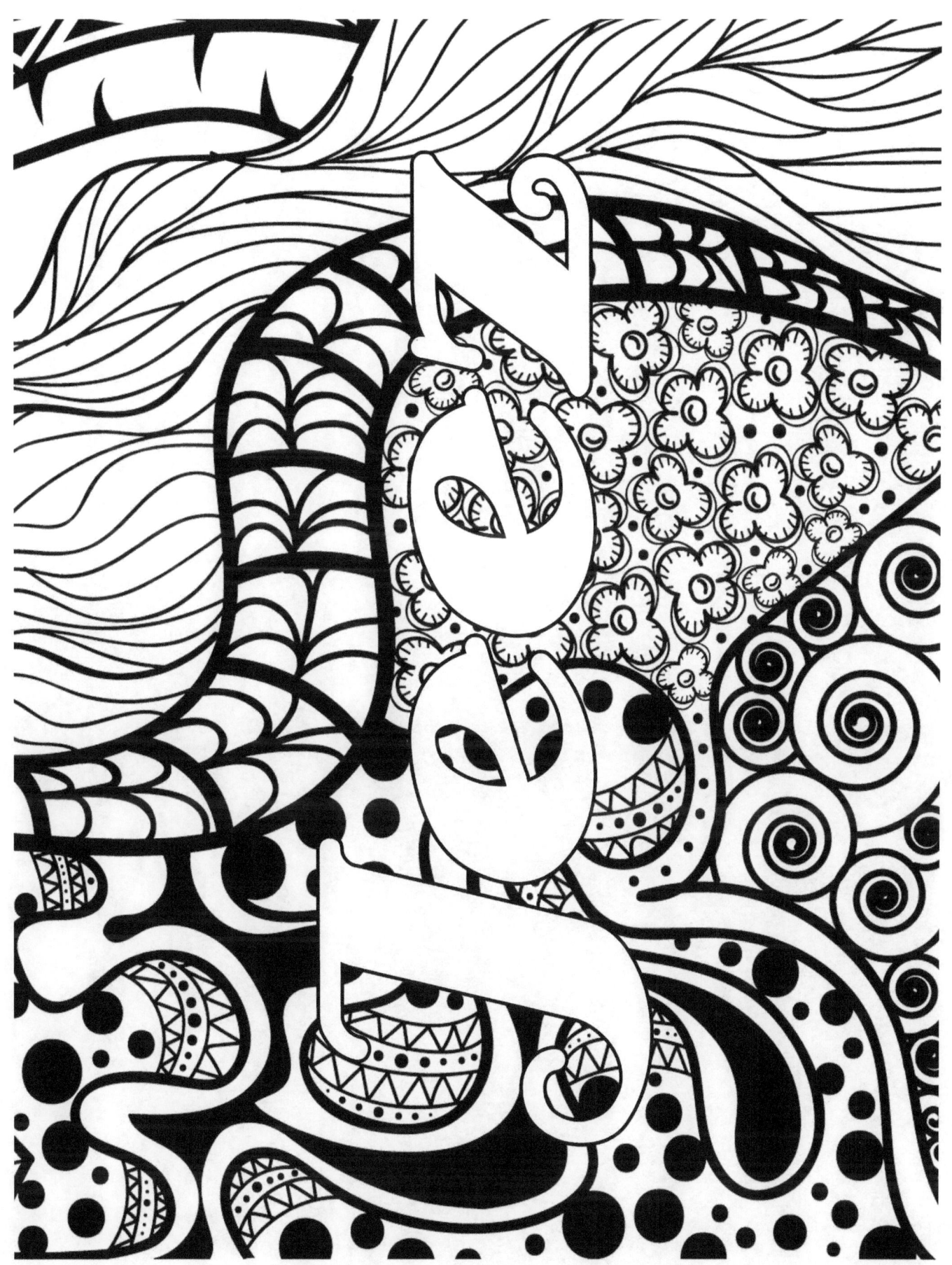

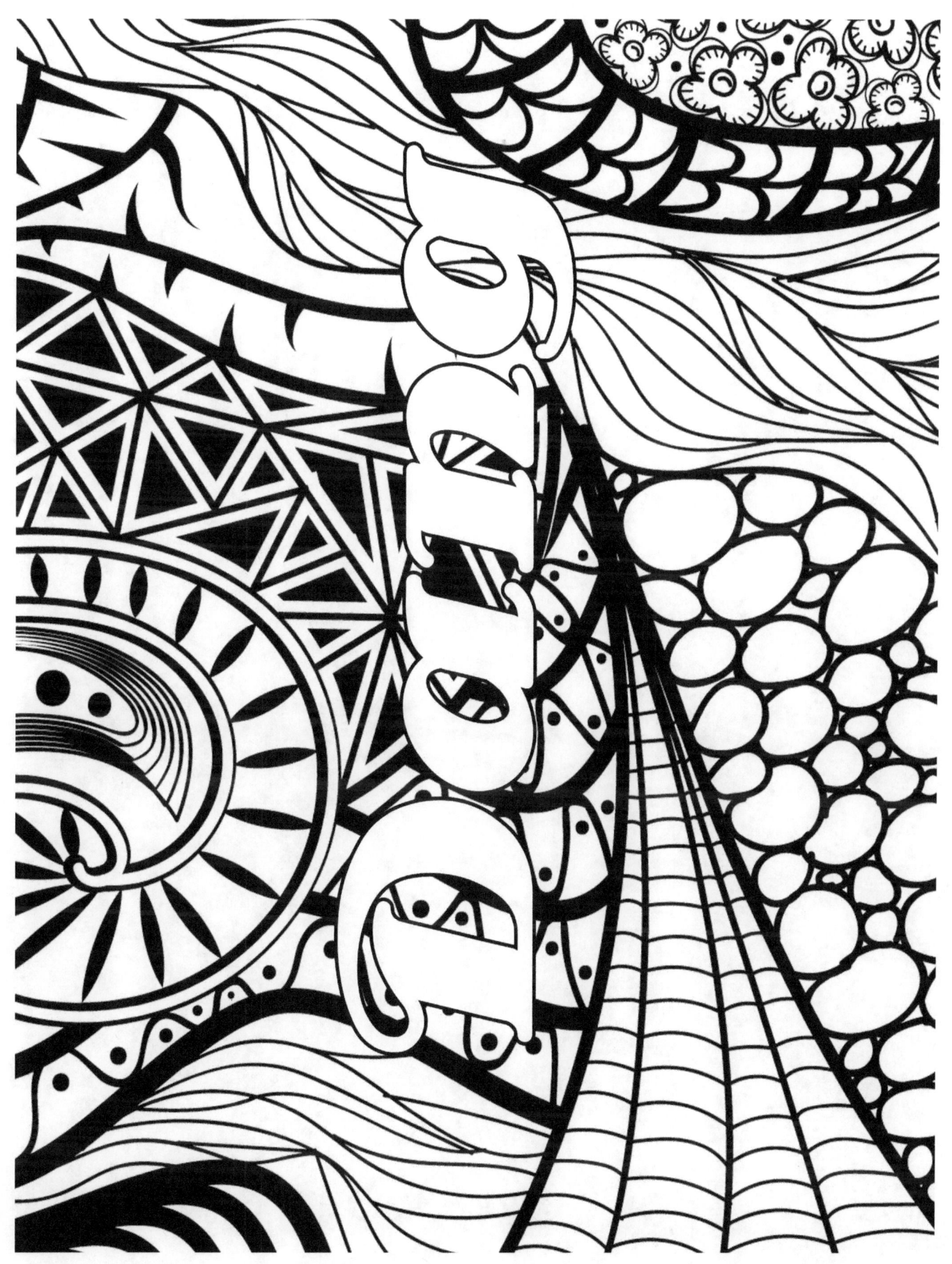

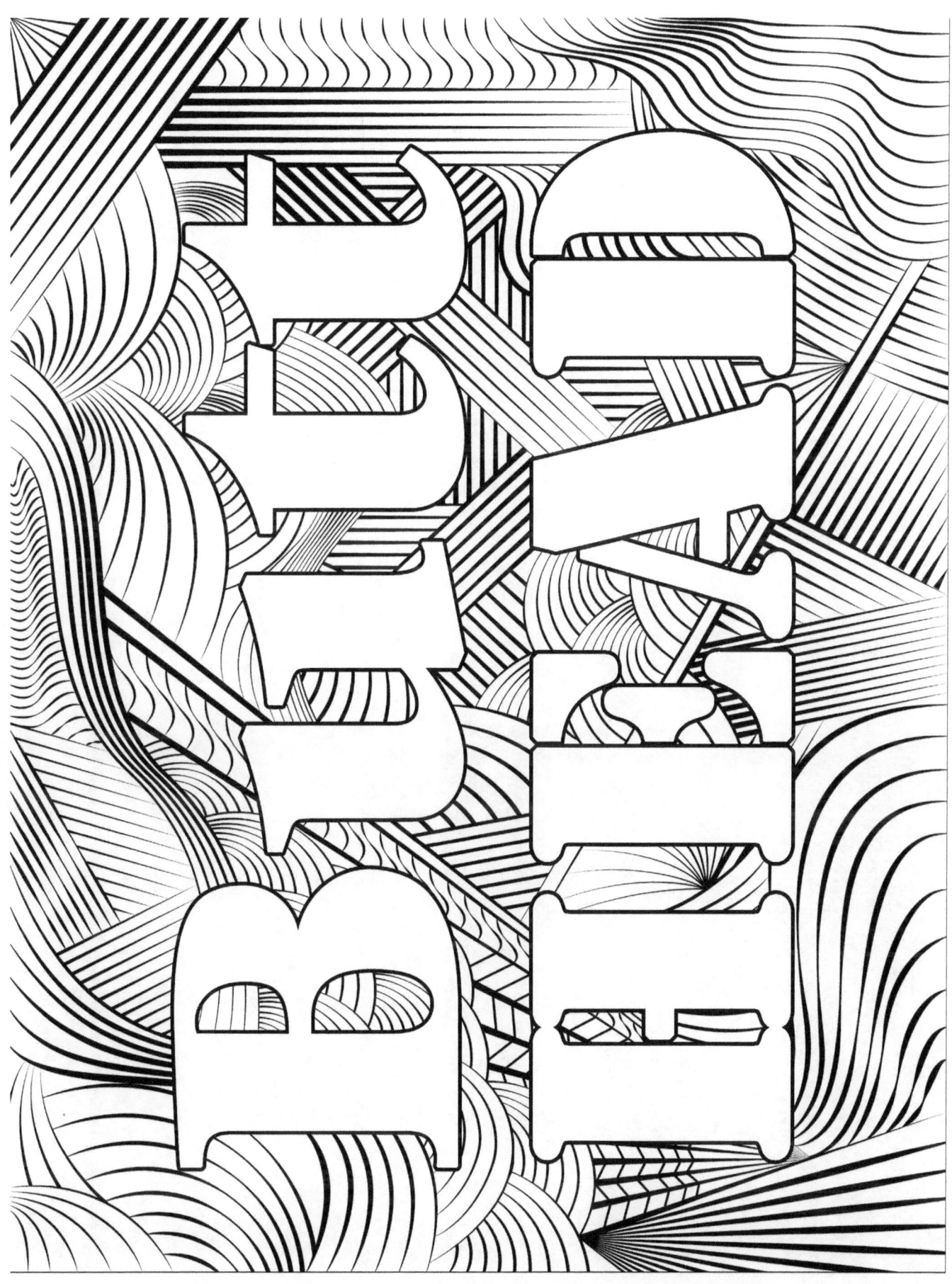

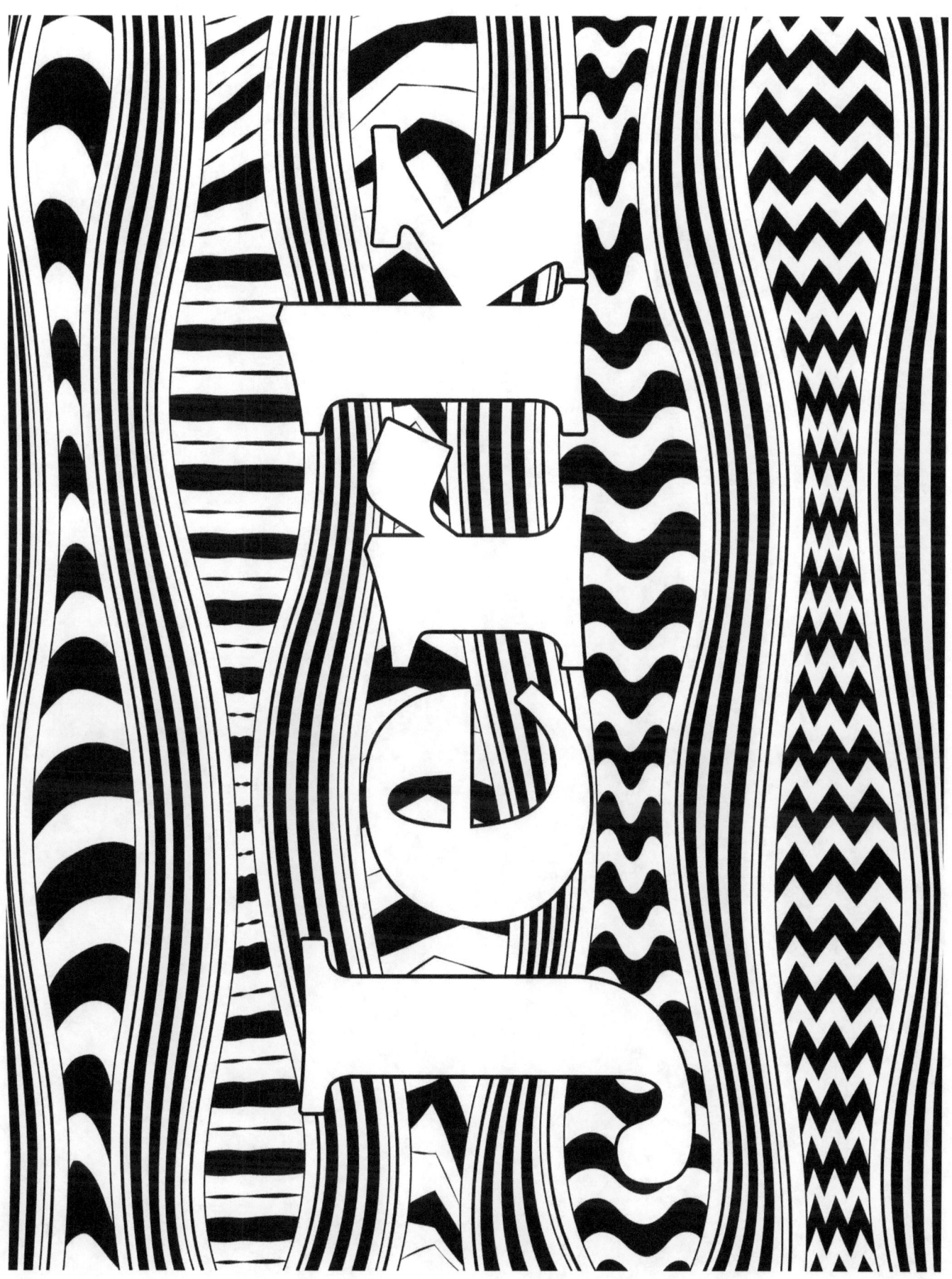

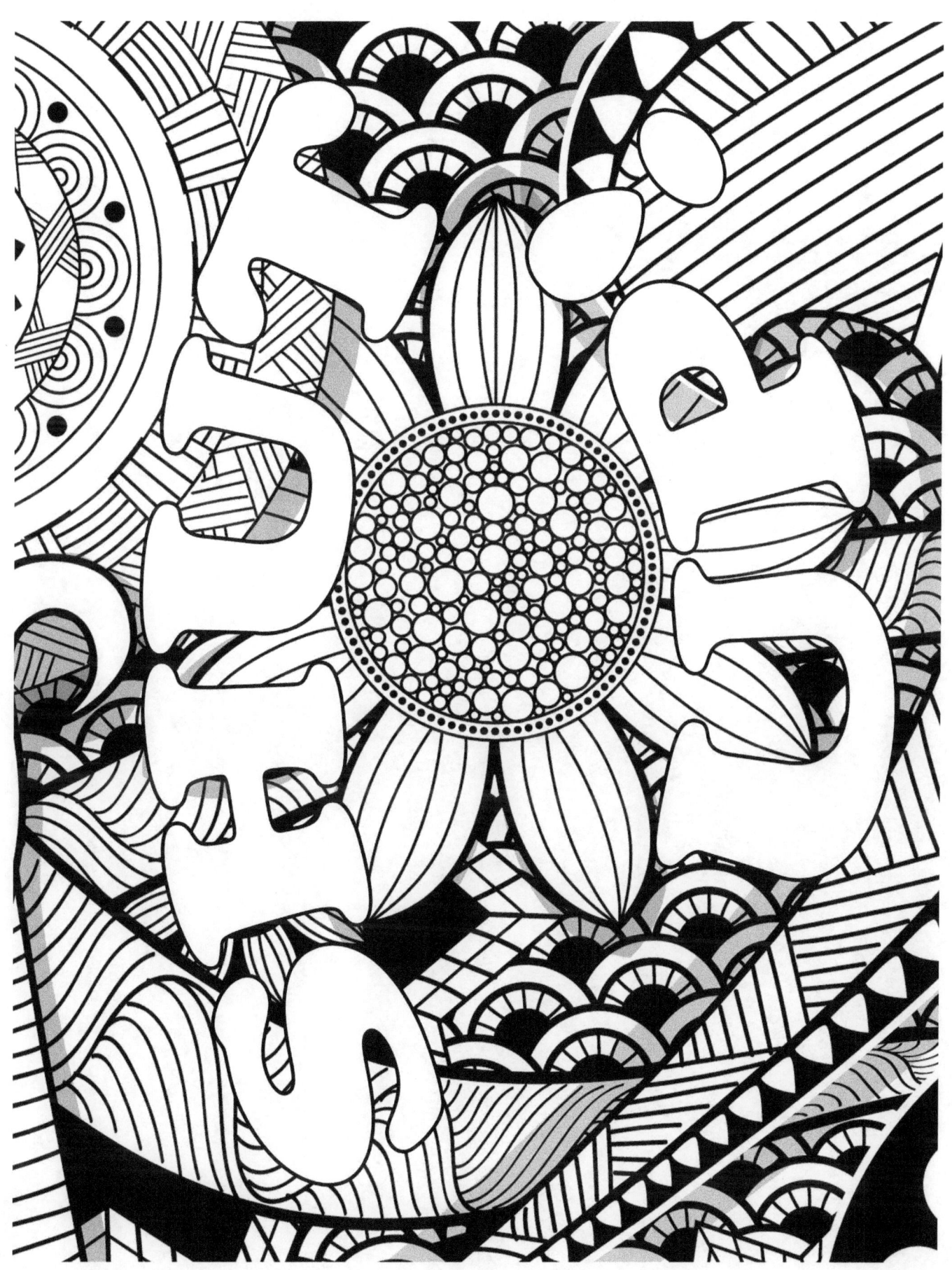

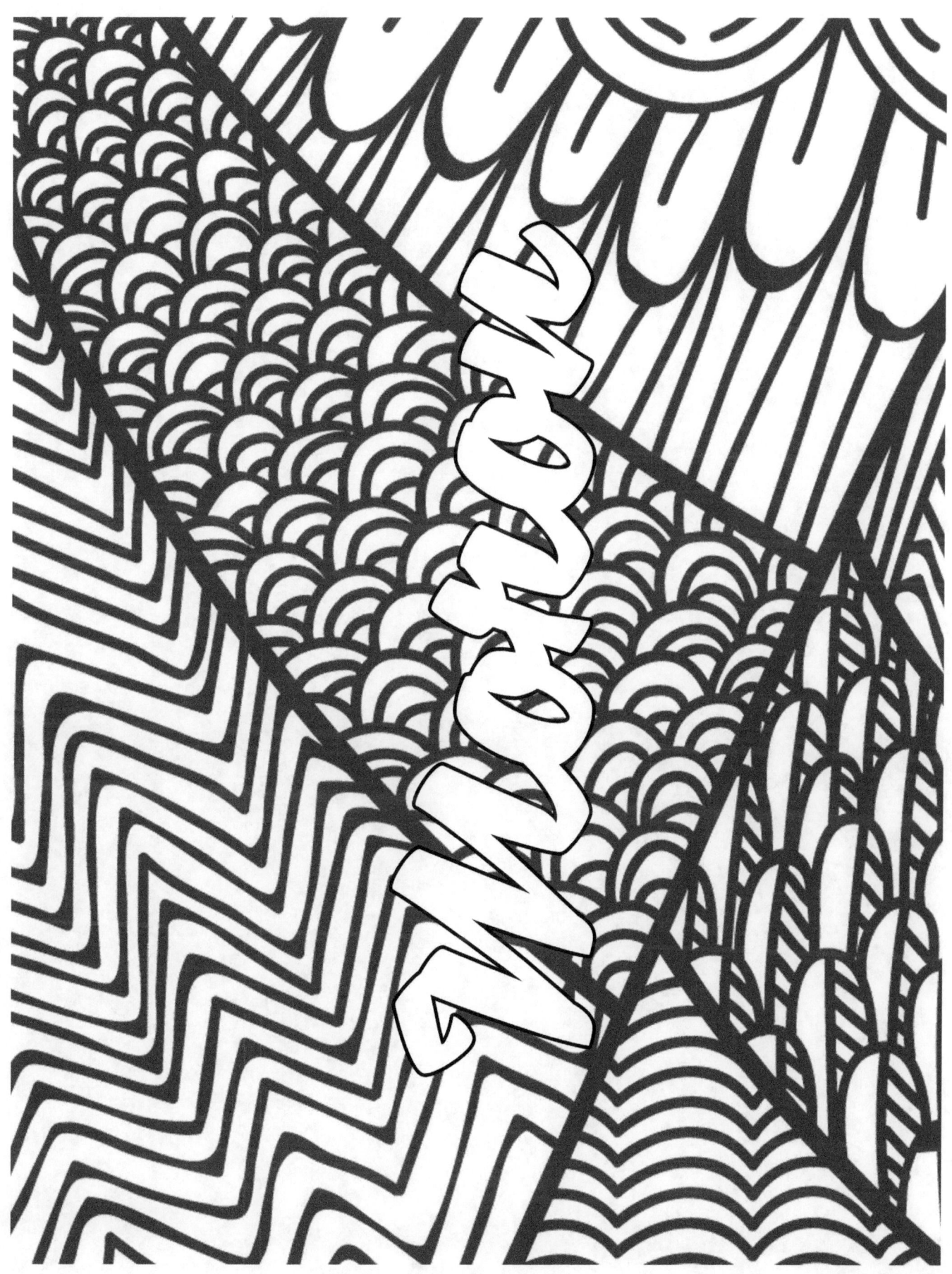

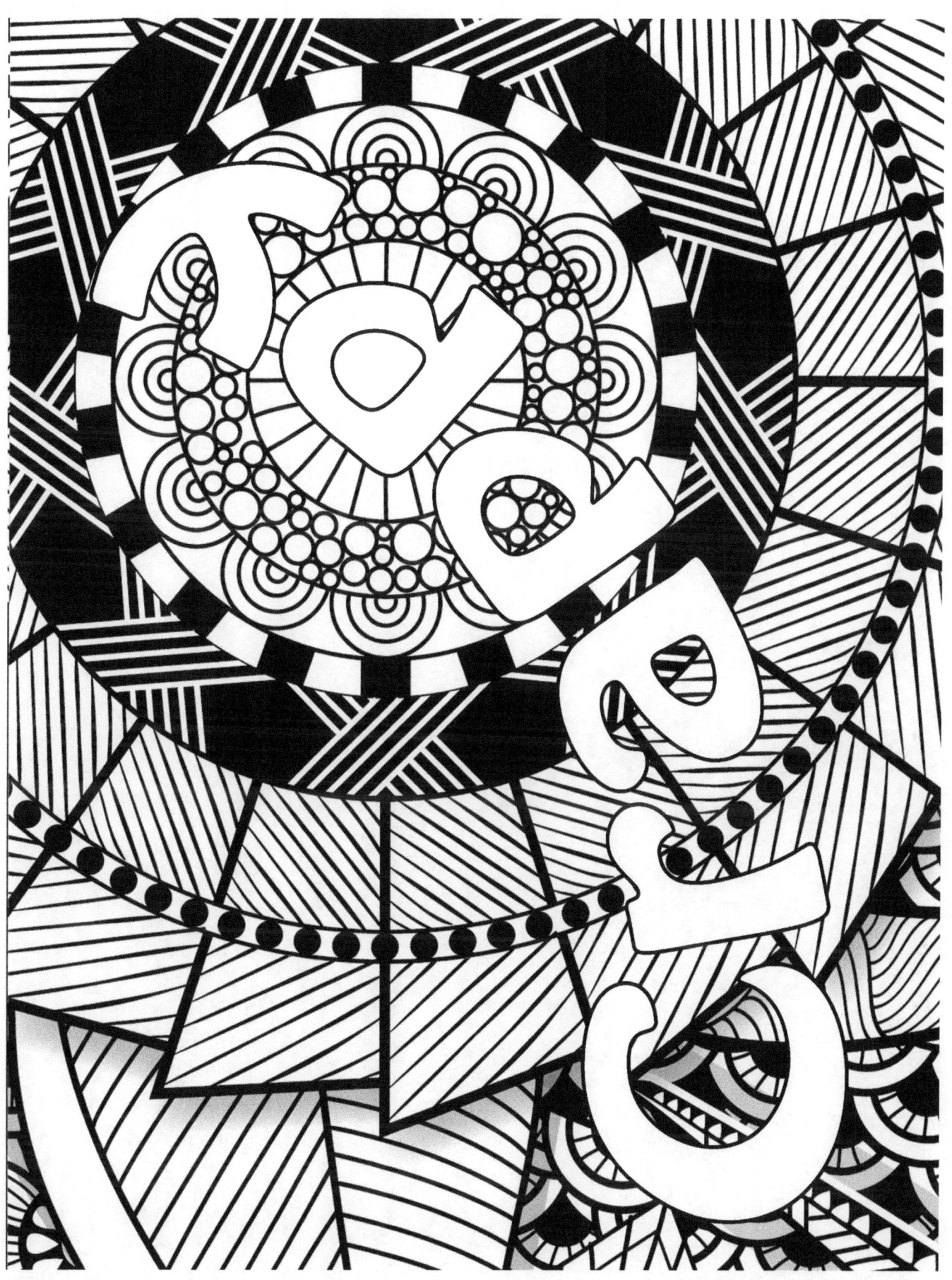

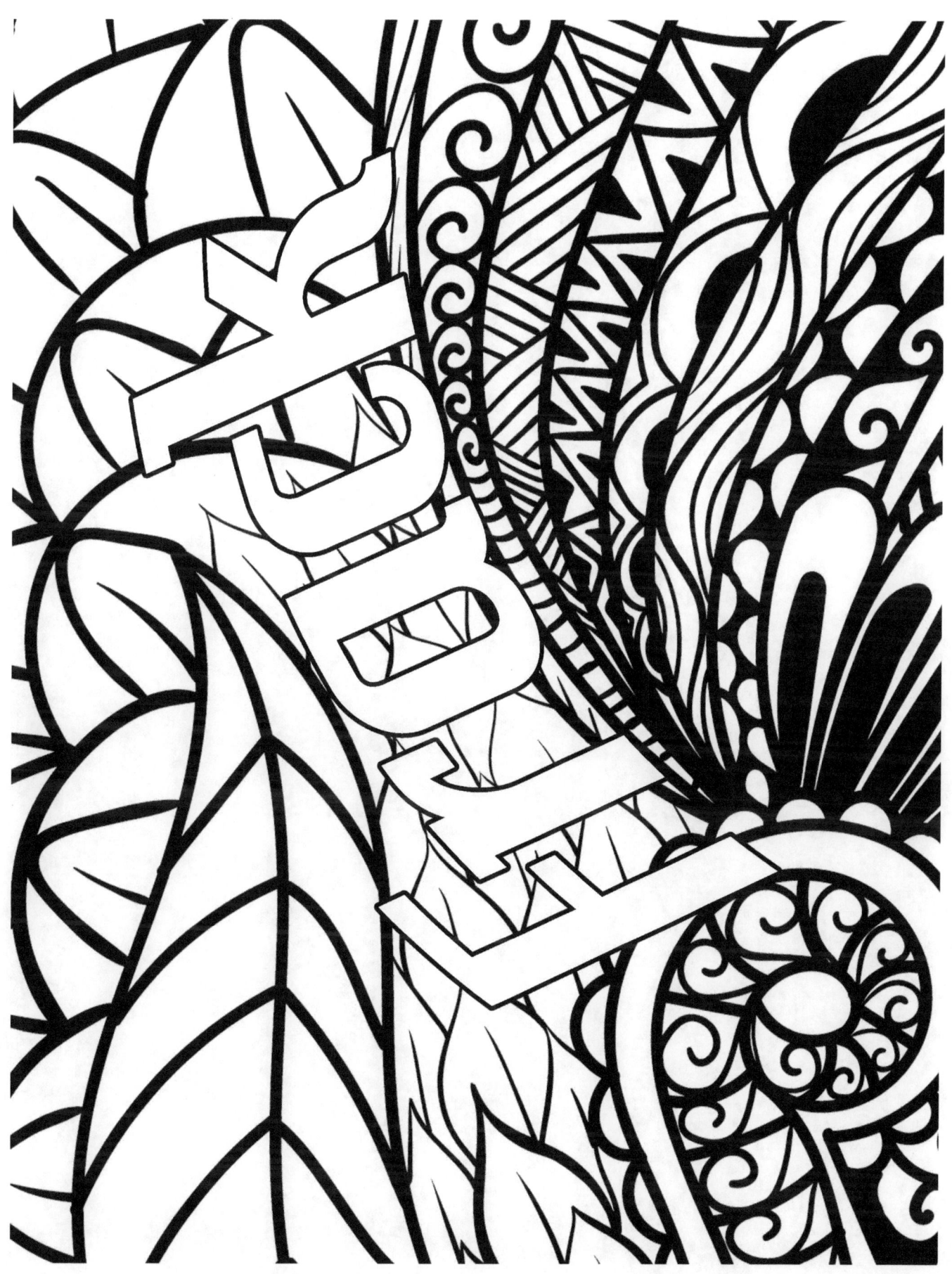

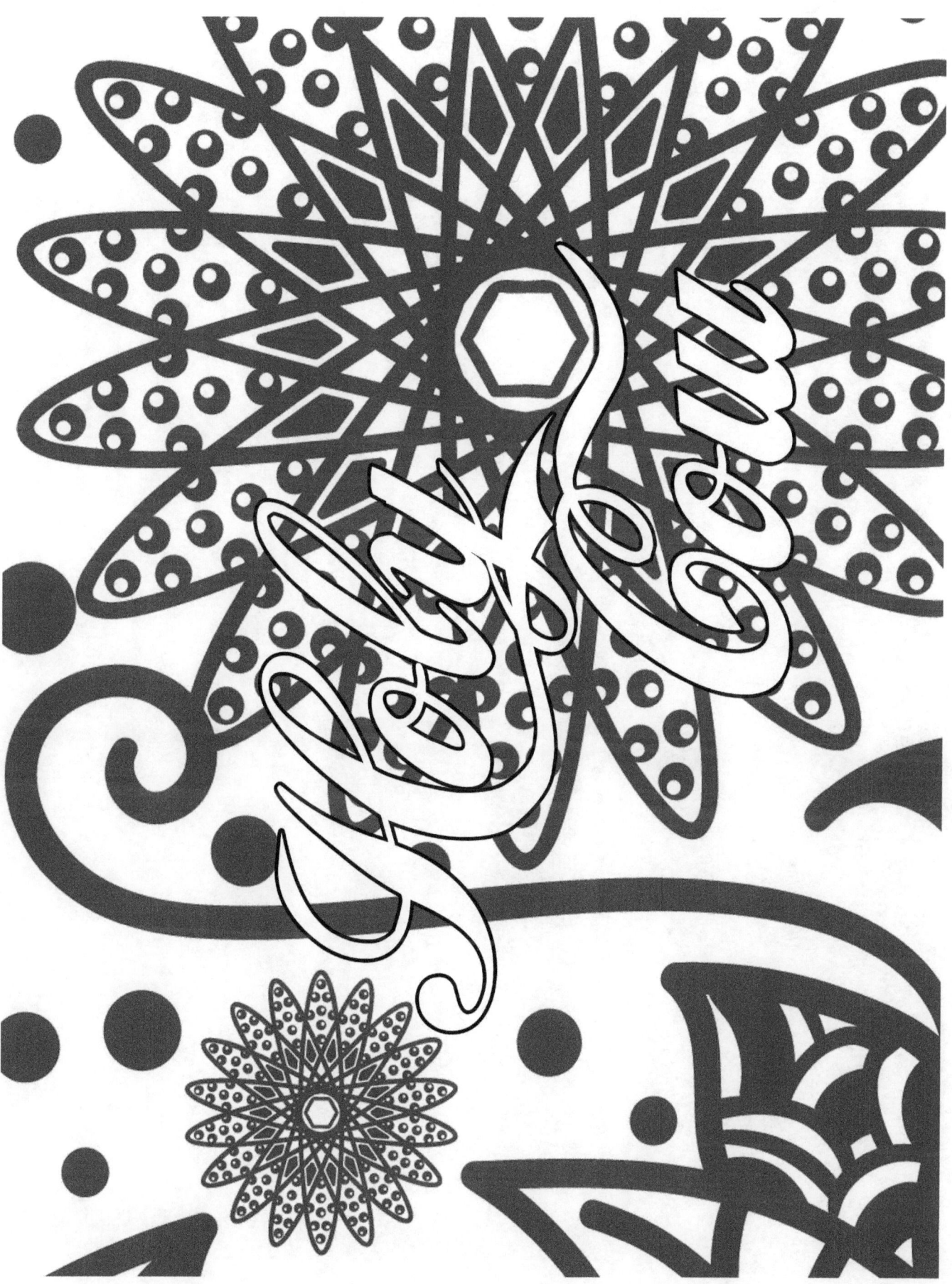

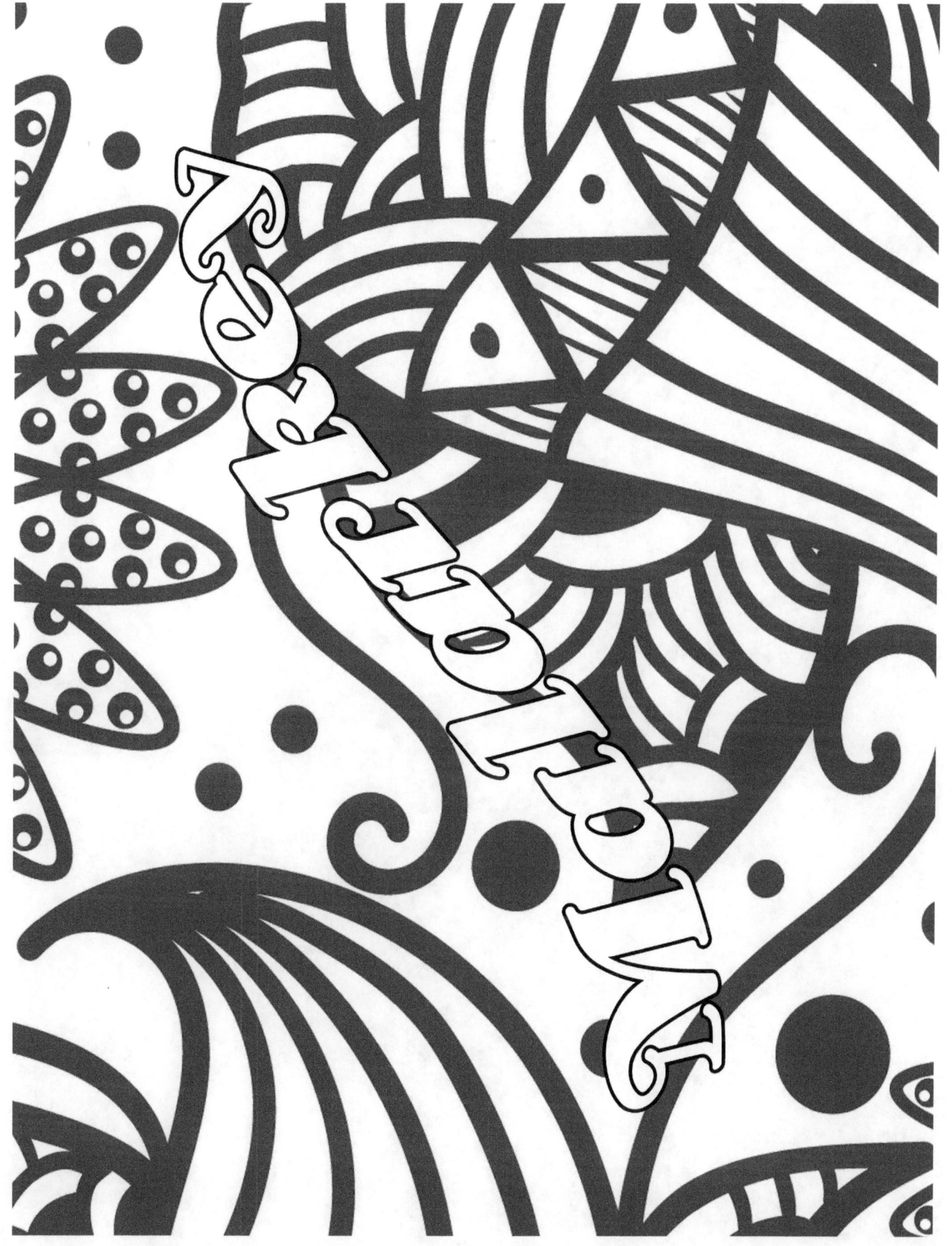

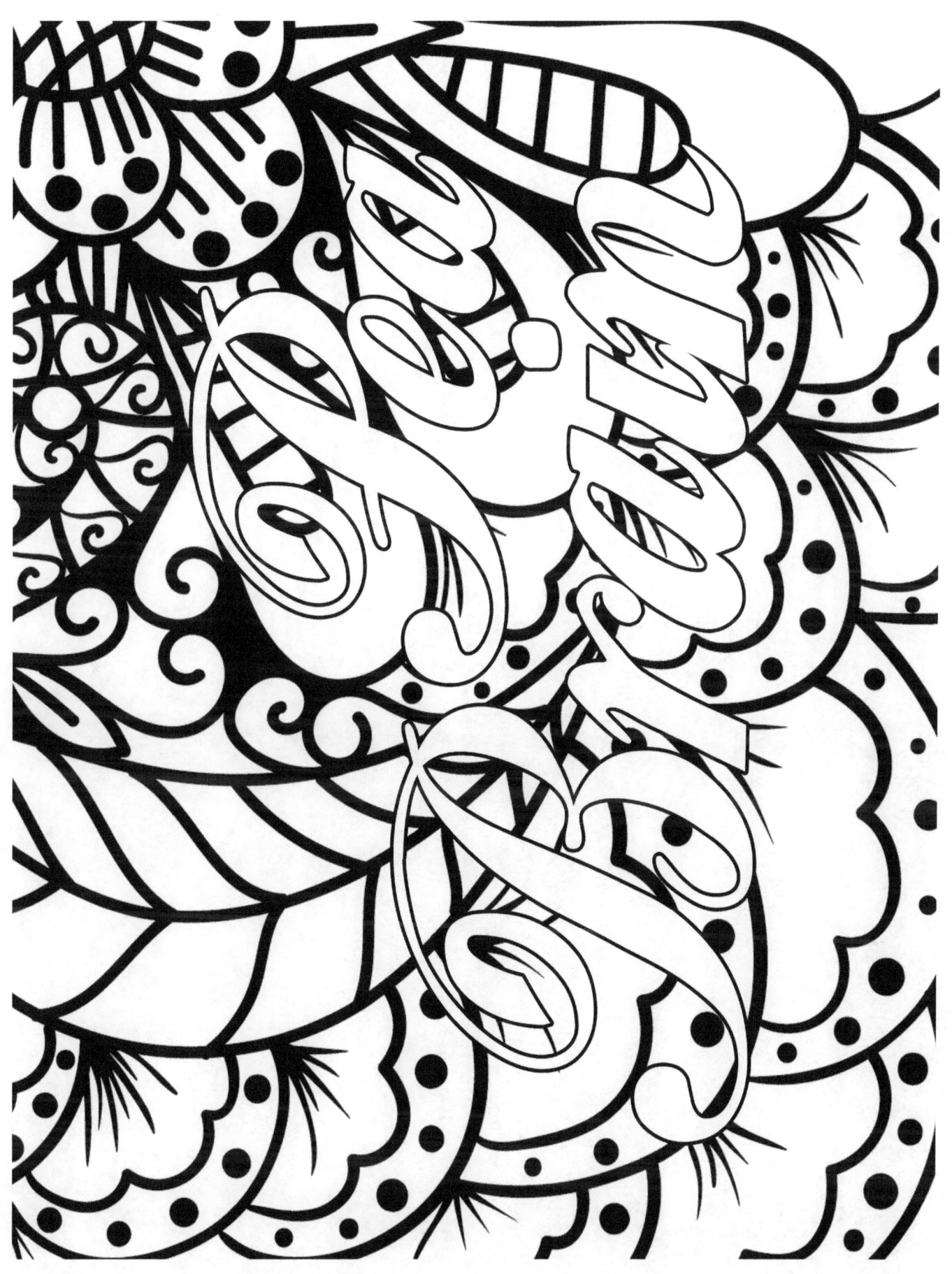

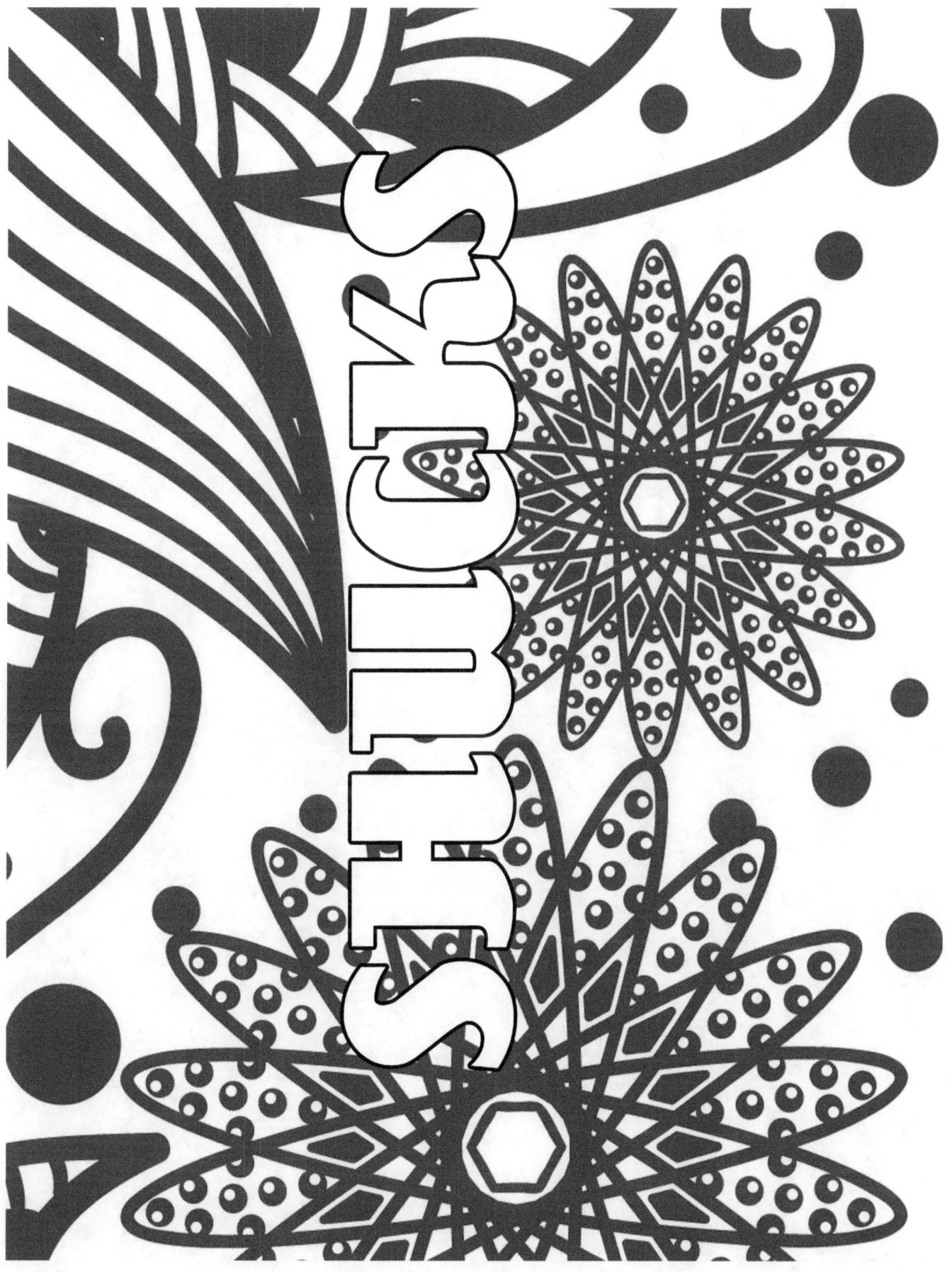

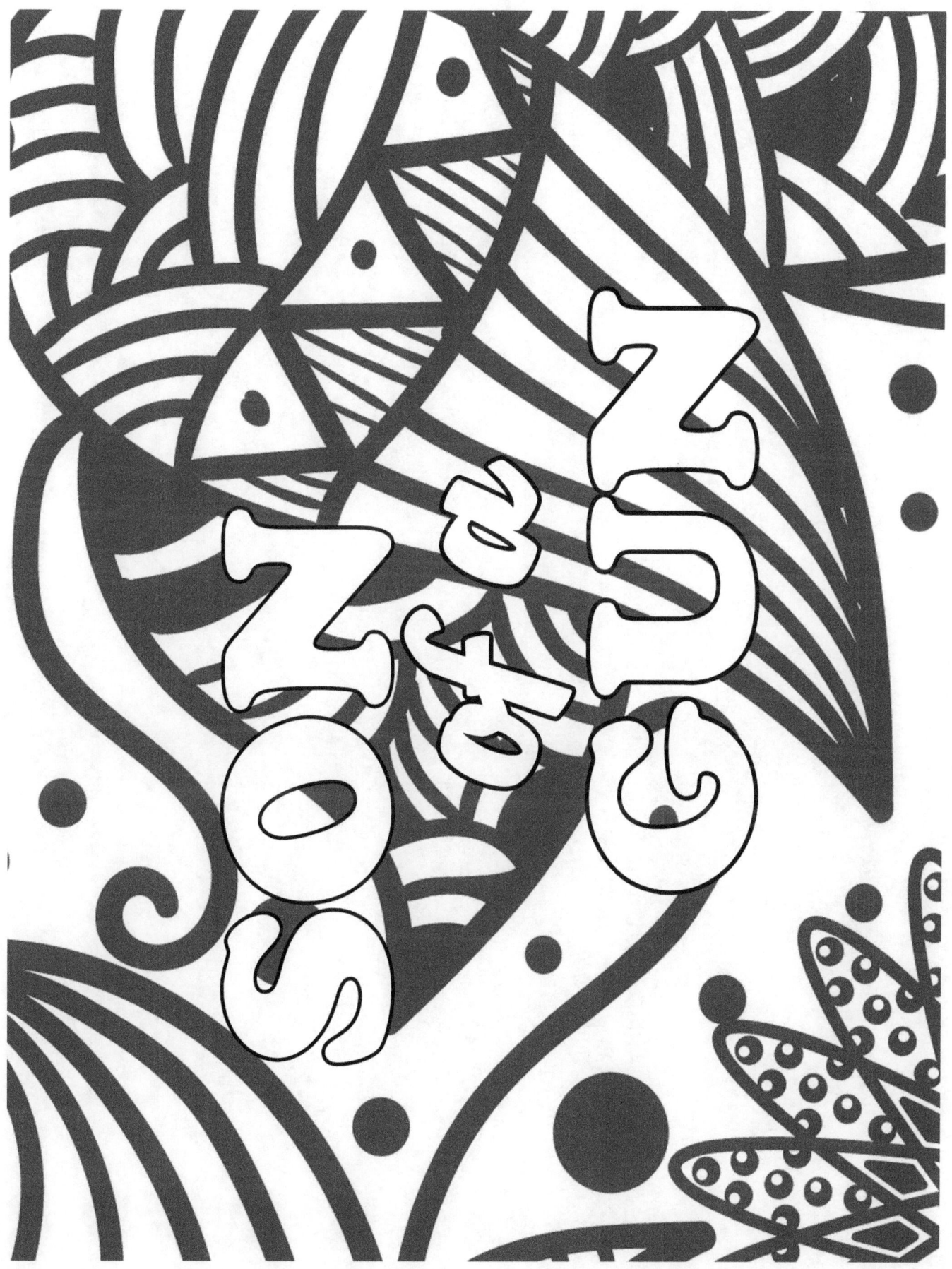

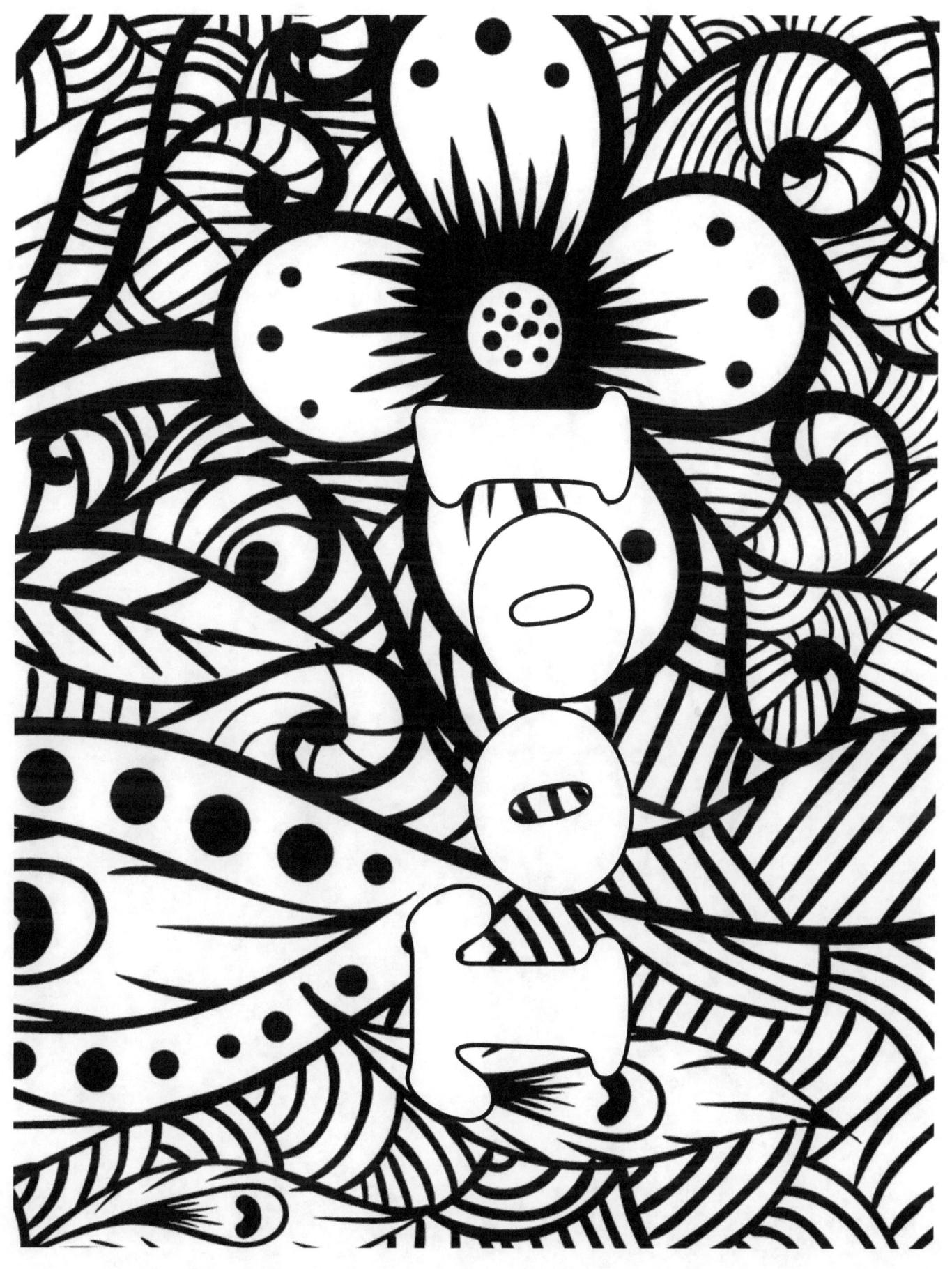

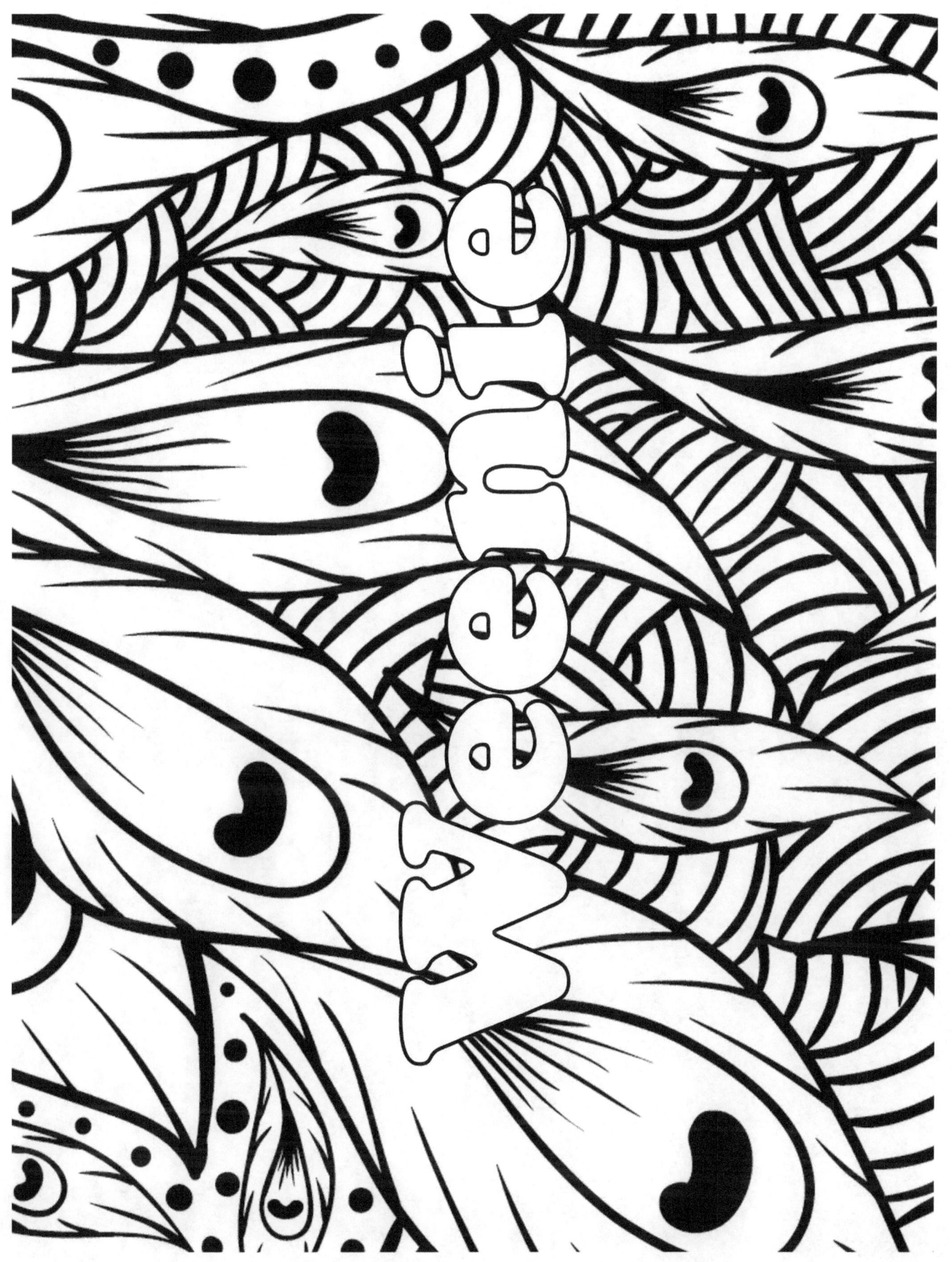

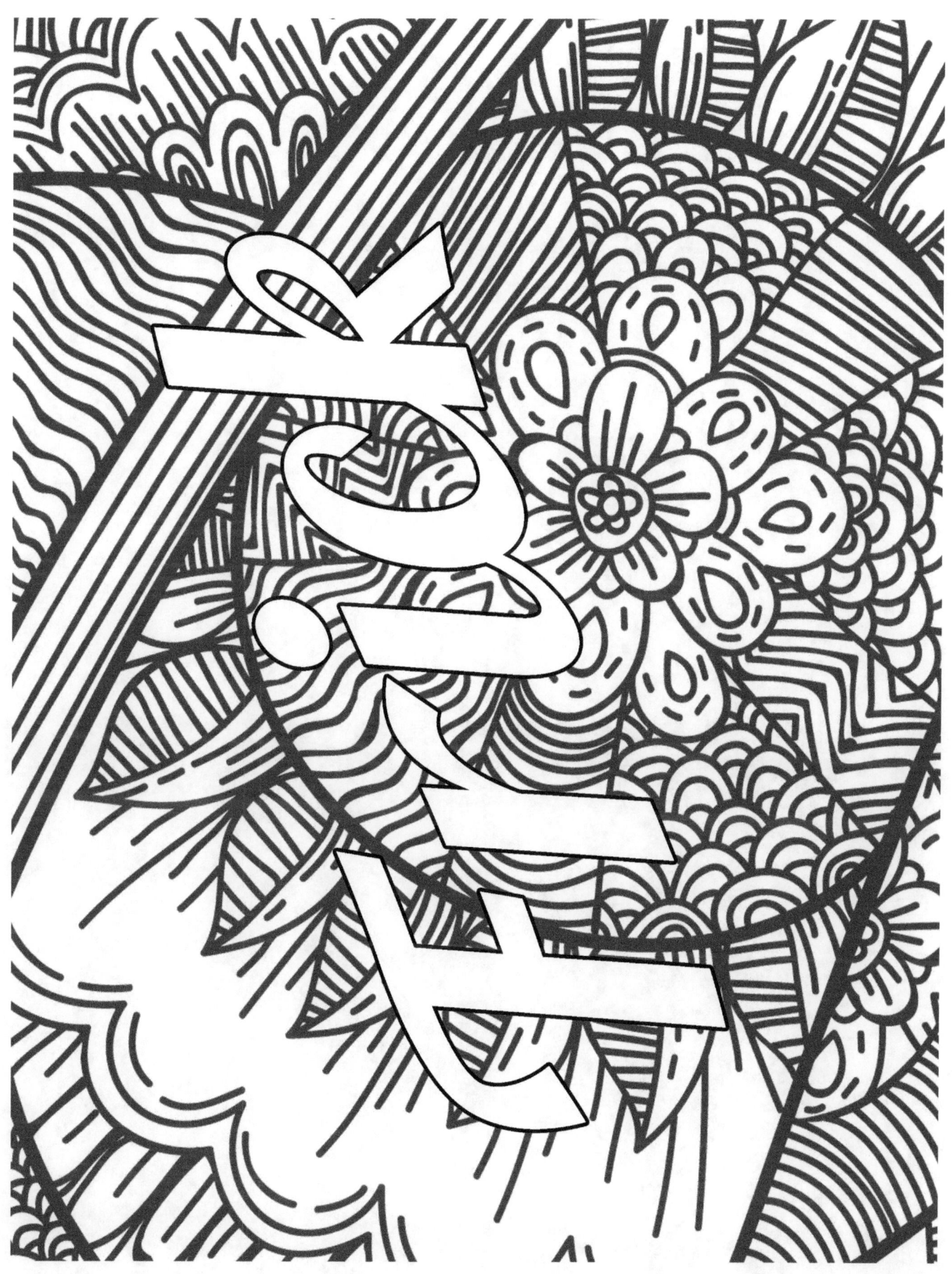

www.ingramcontent.com/pod-product-compliance
Lightning Source LLC
Chambersburg PA
CBHW080629190526
45169CB00009B/3337